D0515562

DISCARD

DISCARD

THE ORANGUTAN

BY STUART P. LEVINE

Endangered Animals & Habitats

SAN LEANDRO LIBRARY HIGH SCHOOL

LUCENT BOOKS, INC.
SAN DIEGO, CALIFORNIA

Look for these and other books in the
Lucent Endangered Animals and Habitats Series:

The Amazon Rain Forest
The Bald Eagle
The Bear
Birds of Prey
Coral Reefs
The Elephant
The Giant Panda
The Gorilla
The Manatee

The Oceans
The Orangutan
The Rhinoceros
Seals and Sea Lions
The Shark
The Tiger
The Whale
The Wolf

Library of Congress Cataloging-in-Publication Data

Levine, Stuart P., 1968–
    The orangutan / by Stuart P. Levine.
        p.   cm. — (Endangered animals & habitats) (Lucent
overview series)
    Includes bibliographical references (p.) and index.
    Summary: Discusses the physical characteristics, behavior,
habitats, and endangered status of the orangutan.
    ISBN 1-56006-560-5 (lib. bdg. : alk. paper)
    1. Orangutan—Juvenile literature. 2. Endangered species—
Juvenile literature. [1. Orangutan 2. Endangered species.]
I. Title.   II. Series.
QL737.P96L48   2000
599.8'3—dc21

99-37697
CIP

No part of this book may be reproduced or used in any form or by any means, electrical,
mechanical, or otherwise, including, but not limited to, photocopy, recording, or any information storage and retrieval system, without prior written permission from the publisher.

Copyright © 2000 by Lucent Books, Inc.
P.O. Box 289011, San Diego, CA 92198-9011
Printed in the U.S.A.

Contents

Introduction

In THE LAST few decades, there has been ever-increasing interest in the lives and activities of the great apes. Countless documentaries, books, magazine articles, and even major motion pictures have brought people closer to their simian cousins than ever before. Along with this interest has arisen an awareness of the challenges facing their survival. Of all the apes, orangutans are the least studied and least understood. In fact, a recent conference on orangutan conservation even referred to the species as the "neglected ape." Until about twenty-five years ago, neither the scientific community nor the public knew much about orangutans.

Today, the orangutan is at last getting the attention it not only deserves but also desperately needs. In the wild, the red ape, as the orangutan is often called, only exists in isolated pockets on two islands in Southeast Asia: Borneo and Sumatra. Researchers estimate that during the late 1980s and 1990s somewhere between 30 and 50 percent of the wild orangutan population has disappeared. As the new millennium dawns, their numbers stand at less than thirty thousand.

The orangutan has no natural predators. The species is, however, threatened by the world's ever-expanding human population. As the number of people in Southeast Asia grows, there is increasing competition for space. Forests are cleared to create villages and to grow crops. Being the only truly arboreal (tree-dwelling) ape, orangutans are completely dependent on the forest for their survival; over the last twenty years about 80 percent of this habitat has been destroyed. The two nations that govern these islands—Indonesia and Malaysia—are also in serious financial difficulty. A large part of their economy is based on the harvest and sale of timber to the wealthier developed nations of the world. As these trees are removed, the orangutans and other forest inhabitants are running out of places to live.

The orangutan population has greatly decreased in the last fifteen years. Today, it is estimated that there are less than thirty thousand orangutans remaining in the wild.

A more recent problem for the red ape has been poaching. While orangutans are sometimes killed for meat or for trophies, more often they are captured for sale in the illegal pet trade. Since the mid-1980s, owning pet orangutans has been popular in certain Asian countries. The mother orangutans are killed so that poachers can easily scoop up the infant apes, pack them in boxes, and ship them off to a variety of destinations. Orangutans have the slowest reproduction rate of any nonhuman primate species. Consequently, they are slow to recover from such population losses, and this trade in baby orangutans has a serious effect on the survival of the species.

The world's population of orangutans is in serious danger, but there are many efforts under way to help get it back on its feet. Efforts are being made to stop the trade in young orangutans and even recover animals from private homes. These former captives are often rehabilitated and released back into the jungle. Researchers also spend time investigating more efficient and less detrimental methods of farming and timber harvesting to protect the habitat. Captive-breeding programs in zoos are ensuring that, even if the wild population dips below the point of no return, there will always be at least some orangutans left to begin repopulation programs. The question is whether these efforts come too late. Will the human race, which has helped push this ape to the edge of extinction, be willing and able to reverse the damage it has done? It will be no easy task, but the actions of governments, conservationists, scientists, and consumers over the next twenty years will decide the fate of the orangutan.

1

The Red Ape

DESPITE ITS STATUS as one of humankind's closest relatives, the orangutan has been a mystery to scientists until very recently. Although researchers have been studying other apes, such as chimpanzees and gorillas, for over a century, it was not until the late 1960s that they began studying the biology and behavior of orangutans. This may be due, in part, to the more remote habitat of the red ape. Found exclusively on two islands in Southeast Asia, the orangutan has escaped scrutiny for many years.

Over the years many misconceptions have existed about the nature of the red ape. From the seventeenth through the mid–nineteenth century, for example, the animal was known as the "orang outang." Roughly translated as "man of the forest," this title came to be used interchangeably for chimpanzees and gorillas as well, which led to much confusion. Today, when examining notes of nineteenth-century naturalists, it is sometimes difficult to determine whether the traveler was writing about an orangutan, a chimpanzee, or a gorilla.

It is surprising that so little is known about the orangutans, particularly since they are so closely related to humans. According to genetic studies, the orangutan shares approximately 97 percent of its DNA—the building blocks of a living creature's genetic code—with human beings. All monkeys, apes, and humans belong to the same taxonomic order—primates. All primates share certain characteristics, such as movable fingers with nails instead of claws and eyes set in the front of their head for better depth perception. Within this order, there are a number of families. All great apes belong to the family Pongidae.

The earliest ancestor of the pongids was thought to be an apelike creature referred to as *Dryopithecus sivalensis.* Remains of this creature have been found in northern India and Pakistan. Scientists believe that the earliest version of the modern-day orangutan diverged from the rest of the pongids during the Pleistocene and migrated across temporary land bridges toward what is now Indonesia. Fossil records indicate that these orangutans were once widespread and found throughout all of southern Asia. The fossils also show that one ancient type of orangutan, which lived in China, was at least 40 percent larger than the ones alive today. Currently, orangutans (*Pongo pygmaeus*) only exist in the wild on the islands of Borneo and Sumatra, which are located just south of Vietnam, Laos, and Cambodia. Scientists assume that the smaller size of these modern-day orangutans was originally an adaptation for island living. In the closed ecological system of an island with no predators, massive size was less important. Likewise, since limited territory was available on an is-

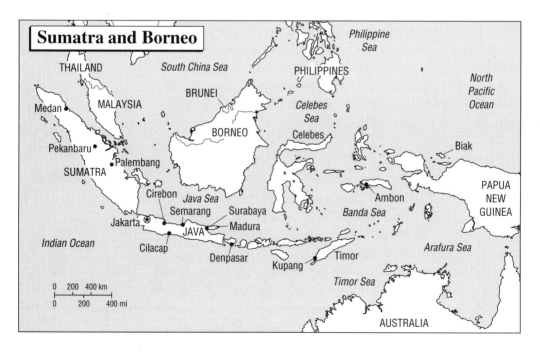

land, being smaller meant that more individuals could survive in that territory.

At one time, orangutans also inhabited the nearby island of Java. However, fossil remains show that these apes disappeared soon after the arrival of a new predator, *Homo erectus,* one of humankind's early ancestors. Researchers agree that these primitive humans made orangutans a large part of their diet, thus forcing the Javan orangutans into extinction. The orangutan species probably owes its modern-day existence to the fact that the more primitive *Homo erectus* never reached the islands of Borneo and Sumatra. To a lesser extent, modern humans (*Homo sapiens*) also consumed orangutans as part of their diet. This is evidenced by the charred orangutan bones that were found in the thirty-five-thousand-year-old *Homo sapiens* cave dwellings on Borneo. *Homo sapiens,* however, appear to have depended more heavily on agriculture than their predecessors did and, consequently, may have had less of an impact on the orangutan population.

A tale of two orangutans

Scientists consider the orangutans of Sumatra and Borneo to be two separate subspecies. This means that they are very similar and can interbreed, but they have a few distinctive traits that are unique to their area of origin. According to John Mackinnon, a well-known orangutan researcher, Sumatran orangutans (*Pongo pygmaeus abelii*) have lighter colored coats and white or yellow hair around their faces. Bornean orangutans (*Pongo pygmaeus pygmaeus*) have darker chocolate or maroon coats. There are also noticeable differences in the facial structure of adult Sumatran and Bornean males. Both have flaps of skin on the sides of their face, which are called cheek flaps or flanges. The Sumatran's flanges are less pronounced and outline the entire face, creating a diamond shape. However, the Bornean's flanges are larger and tend to hang downward, drooping off the face and creating a square appearance. Male Sumatran orangutans also have longer, fuller beards and a soft coat of hair on their flanges while Bornean males have sparse, thick

Although both are members of the same species, orangutans from Sumatra (left) can be distinguished from those on Borneo (right) by their facial features and the color of their coats.

hairs on their flanges. Though not conclusively proven, many orangutan researchers believe that the Sumatran is slightly more social than the Bornean. These assumptions are based primarily on studies of captive orangutans, but recent research from the wild seems to support the theory.

Habitat

According to a recent survey by the International Union for the Conservation of Nature and Natural Resources (IUCN), one of the world's leaders in conservation research, current estimates put the population of orangutans on Borneo at somewhere between ten and sixteen thousand. They have been observed living throughout the island, which is divided into four basic regions. Kalimantan, a province of the country of Indonesia, is the largest area and is home to most of the orangutans on the island. Sabah and Sarawak are considerably smaller states and are part of the nation of Malaysia. These two areas are home to a number of orangutans, and much new research is being done there. The final area is a tiny region known as Brunei. This independent nation is home to a small number of orangutans. In fact, sightings have been sparse and not well documented, leading scientists to believe that they may be near extinction in this particular region.

The island of Sumatra, which is entirely governed by Indonesia, only has orangutans in one localized region, called Atjeh, in the northwestern part of the island. Almost all the orangutans on Sumatra live in or near the Greater Leuser area, which encompasses the Gunung Leuser National Park and its surroundings. The most recent estimates for the Sumatran orangutan population stand at seven to twelve thousand.

All of the great apes spend some time in trees, but orangutans are the only ones that spend the bulk of their lives there. In fact, they are the largest primarily arboreal animals on earth. They depend completely on the trees for their survival. They spend most of their days and nights traveling, foraging, and sleeping in the branches of the trees. They have been observed to live in a variety of forested regions, from swamps and lowlands to hills and mountains. Orangutans do not usually live in areas higher than fifty-four hundred feet above sea level, however, because the types of foods they eat do not grow at higher altitudes.

Physiology

An orangutan's size makes for a precarious life up in the rain forest canopy, often more than fifty feet above the ground. A male orangutan can reach a maximum size of two hundred pounds; the female will typically be closer to one hundred pounds. Orangutans, however, are built with a number of seemingly useful adaptations for life in the trees. Their fantastic coordination; slow, methodical style of movement; long arms; and dexterous, hooklike hands all make it possible for them to maneuver safely through the trees.

Unlike other great apes, the orangutan spends most of its life in the trees.

In addition to their build and agility, orangutans have another physical adaptation to life in the trees. Humans and most primates can rotate their arms in a full arc. Orangutans, due to the absence of a certain ligament, have this same rotational flexibility in their legs. This gives the orangutan the equivalent of four arms. Since they are too bulky to jump from branch to branch, they use their incredibly long arms, which can spread to a width of nearly seven feet, to maneuver delicately through the forest canopy. Their dexterous hands and feet all have opposable thumbs, which allow them the convenience of a four-handed grip wherever they go. They can even use their massive size to their advantage by weighing down a branch or an entire tree, moving it in whatever direction they please, and then using it as a bridge to the next tree on their path. While hanging from a suspended branch, they will carefully move only one hand or foot at a time. This apparent sluggishness is actually a survival adaptation for life in the trees. A wrong step would make for a long fall to the ground. In fact, researchers have found that older, heavier males often spend more of their later years on the ground since they can no longer maneuver their mass through the trees.

Diet and feeding

One possible reason why orangutans spend so much of their lives in the trees is because this is where they find most of their food. Orangutans are primarily frugivores, or fruit eaters. According to Peter S. Rodman, an anthropologist at the University of California at Davis, orangutans' diets consist of 53 percent fruit. The other 47 percent is made up of mostly leaves and bark as well as the occasional insect and small mammal. Fruit appears to be their food of choice, and they will only resort to other items when fruit is unavailable. Researchers have cataloged over four hundred types of fruit on their menu. These include many different types of plums and figs as well as a number of more exotic fruits such as litchis, rambutans, *taraps, lansats, merang, kubriz,* and *pintau.* One of their favorite fruits, however, is the durian. People who have sampled durian report that it tastes like butter almond ice cream. However, getting at the tasty meat of the fruit is no easy task. The fruit itself is heavy, weighing almost three pounds, and it is covered with a layer of sharp

 ## The Mental Map

Orangutans have often been referred to as the botanists of the animal world because they have an uncanny ability to locate any type of ripened fruit, no matter its location or unusual growth cycle. Some of the trees on which they depend may only produce fruit once every four or five months while others may take as long as several years. To make matters more complicated, unlike temperate forests, their rain forest habitat does not cluster similar species of trees. To find a particular fruit, orangutans may have to travel a mile or more. Each orangutan seems to possess a detailed mental map of where specific types of fruit are and when they are in season and ripe. They may eat a particularly favored fruit for part of a day and then deliberately travel a great distance to another tree of the same species to find more of the same ripe fruit they were enjoying. The cognitive implications of these abilities have led researchers to investigate the intelligence and problem-solving capacities of orangutans in captivity.

The orangutan possesses an amazing ability to locate any kind of ripened fruit in its territory.

spikes, making it quite cumbersome to tote around in the treetops. Its shell is so hard that only a full-grown orangutan can pry it open. The task requires strength, perseverance, and a delicate touch to avoid being impaled by a spike.

The majority of orangutans' waking hours are spent in the pursuit of food. They are constantly moving to follow the ever-shifting cycle of ripening fruits and flowering plants upon which they feed. Studies have shown orangutans to be extremely intelligent creatures. Researchers be-

Birute Galdikas, a pioneer in orangutan research, plays with a pair of young orangutans.

lieve that a large part of their considerable cognitive, or mental, abilities are dedicated to remembering the exact location and growth cycles of each of the thousands of sparsely distributed fruit sources within their home range. Birute Galdikas, one of the pioneers of orangutan research, refers to them as "the most brilliant botanists on the planet."[1] Each stop on their endless journey may only yield a few bites of some desired food, so they cannot afford to waste any time or energy in unsuccessful searches for food. Consequently, this mental map of their environment is critical to their survival.

Social structure

The sparse distribution of food makes it impractical for orangutans to live in large groups. Indeed, orangutans differ from most primates in that they have few tight social bonds with others of their species, except for the temporary association of the mother and her offspring. Until recently, orangutans were thought to be completely solitary animals, spending nearly their entire lives alone, uninterested in the affairs of any other creatures. It has come to light, however, that they do have a loosely structured social network, but that they simply do not live in close proximity to one another or depend on each other's presence for comfort or survival.

There are a number of reasons for this unusual lifestyle. The primary reason that any animals live together in groups is for the mutual benefit of safety in numbers. By living together, they increase their chances of survival from predators. However, this group living also causes some competition and aggression between animals within the community. Among more social primates, there are continuous squabbles over food resources and breeding privileges. An adult orangutan, on the other hand, has no natural predators on either Borneo or Sumatra. Therefore, it does not require the protection afforded by living in a community. Solitary life, therefore, appears to be an adaptation to the orangutan's environment.

Territory

*Adolescent female
orangutans often form
small temporary
groups.*

Each adult orangutan, whether male or female, occupies a home range, or territory, that it defends against unwelcome intruders. It is in this one area that an orangutan will live its entire life—eating, breeding, and, in the case of females, raising its young. Females occupy much smaller territories than males, and they often overlap with other females.

Adolescent female orangutans often form small temporary groups.

Despite their generally solitary nature, adolescent females will often form small groups before they are old enough to establish firm territories of their own. These groups will stay together for several days or even weeks at a time. In some cases, these brief but often-repeated associations form the basis for lifelong friendships. As adults, female orangutans will readily recognize friends and on occasion travel together for a few hours or even a few days. They also seem to recognize other orangutans whom they have not gotten along with in the past, and they make obvious efforts to avoid them. When two females do come together, they appear to use a subtle repertoire of facial expressions, body postures, and vocalizations to greet or communicate with each other. According to Birute Galdikas, these expressions are far too subtle for the casual observer to notice; thus, orangutans have been wrongly labeled as impassive and unemotive. Instead of participating in the demonstrative displays used by other apes, they seem content to simply sit in each other's company and enjoy the companionship for short periods of time.

Male territory

A male orangutan's territory is much larger than a female's and typically overlaps that of several females. Males are far more solitary than females. They rarely come into contact with other adult males, and they never travel together, even for short periods. Similar to other primates, male orangutans do have a dominance hierarchy, but unlike other apes, they maintain it despite little or no contact with each other. Each male has a distinct vocalization, known as a "long call." An orangutan uses this to alert other males in the area to his presence. Although the apes rarely even see each other, they each appear to remember which call belongs to which orangutan. Depending on the individual's rank in the local hierarchy, others hearing that call will either give way or continue toward it, sounding off with their own long calls. On the rare occasions when they do come into contact, they will usually create a commotion, often threatening, vocalizing, and attempting to determine who should give way, all without physical contact. However, when two individuals of similar rank square off, neither may yield. A fight then occurs in which they will grab, bite, yell, and attempt to knock each other to the forest floor. While such fights can look very dangerous, serious injury or death rarely occurs.

Courtship

Female orangutans differ from other apes in that they do not have a distinguishable estrous cycle. They do have a menstrual cycle, but it is more similar to a human female's. Orangutans have no outward signs that they are ovulating, and they do not restrict their sexual receptivity to any one phase of their menstrual cycle, although they do copulate more often during ovulation. They are, however, picky about with whom they will mate. Females seem to give preferential treatment to the largest, strongest males in their local region.

When a female decides to willingly consort with a male, she makes her intent very plain. In this case, the female is often the aggressor. She will follow the male she is interested in for days, if necessary, to gain his attention. They will feed and travel together for an extended period, copulating frequently. It is only during these extended courtships that the female may become pregnant. Long-term studies have shown that these same couples appear to come together repeatedly. By breeding with the same female over

Unwanted Advances

Female orangutans are very picky when choosing a mate. They typically seem to want the largest, strongest males. A male usually does not reach his full size until about age fifteen. However, he is sexually mature by the age of nine or ten. For this reason, males are usually unsuccessful in their attempts to attract females during this subadult phase. While a ten-year-old male may not be big enough to elicit a favorable response from a female, he is still considerably larger and stronger than most full-grown females. The young male's strength allows him to force his attentions on the females when they are unresponsive to his advances. This is usually the only way that subadult males can mate. According to researchers, pregnancy never occurs as a result of these nonconsensual liaisons.

Female orangutans almost always choose only the largest and strongest males as mates.

several seasons, the male increases the chances that the offspring he later sees her with is his. Male orangutans are very territorial and rarely allow another male in their home range. As a male infant grows to be a juvenile, the local adult male is more likely to tolerate the presence of a male that is his offspring.

Birth and growth

After conception has taken place, the male orangutan has little to do with the care and raising of the young. The female, on the other hand, takes an enormous amount of responsibility for her young, expending huge amounts of energy in their care over a period of several years. In addition to nourishing and protecting the youngster, she must teach it all of the skills it will need to survive in the world. Orangutans breed and grow very slowly compared to most other primates. They have an interbirth interval of five to eight years, which appears to be an adaptation to their lengthy rearing process.

Few orangutan births have been observed in the wild. Researcher Galdikas reportedly followed a pregnant female for an extended period and was able to witness the birth process from a safe distance. A day or so before the orangutan gave birth, she stopped feeding and climbed approximately seventy feet up a tree. She constructed a nest for herself and in a few hours gave birth to what Galdikas estimated to be a two-pound baby. The mother was observed inspecting the infant and stretching the limbs out systematically to make sure everything worked correctly.

For the first year, the baby clings to its mother at all times. It does little more than nurse and hang on to her fur during this time. By its first birthday it may weigh fifteen pounds. At this point, it will begin to pick up and eat scraps of food that its mother drops on her belly. By the age of two and a half, the youngster will feed itself independently. At this age, the young orangutan will begin to take quick romps away from its mother.

Young orangutans do not have many playmates due to their mothers' solitary lifestyles. However, on the occasions when mothers meet up and travel with other mother orangutans, the youngsters will play vigorously with each other. These are the

A female orangutan and her baby. For the first year of its life, a baby orangutan will hold fast to its mother's side.

rare opportunities they have to learn how to interact with others of their kind. They still sleep in their mothers' nests until about the age of five, when they will begin to nightly build their own nests right next to their mothers'. Between the ages of six and ten, they begin to look more like adult orangutans. They spend increasing periods of time away from their mothers, often traveling in groups with other orangutans of similar ages. They usually remain in frequent contact with their mothers until age ten. By this time the mothers will probably have given birth to other infants and will have less time to pay attention to their older offspring. The males will then associate with other young males in a bachelor group or will keep to themselves looking to establish territories of their own. The females will usually stay close by for a few more years, watching their mothers care for the newborns. In this way, the females learn the critical skills they will one day need to raise young of their own.

Maturity

A female is considered fully mature and old enough to breed by age seven or eight. They often choose not to mate, however, until age ten or twelve, when they are fully grown and weigh about one hundred pounds.

Males are a little different. At about age nine or ten, they enter a subadult phase. This means that they are no longer immature and are fully capable of breeding, but they do not have the massive size of the adult male. Although they attempt to breed, they are usually shunned by the females. They may travel quite a bit farther from their home range than a female of the same age while trying to establish a new territory of their own. At about age fifteen, males hit a point of rapid maturation. They gain weight, develop the large cheek flanges, their hair becomes longer and darker, and in the case of the Sumatran orangutan, they also grow a long beard. This transition out of the subadult phase can actually be slowed down by the presence of other dominant adult males. It is thought that the presence of these dominating figures not only limits young males' mobility

Orang Pendek

North America has Bigfoot, or Sasquatch. The Himalayas have the Abominable Snowman, or Yeti. The island of Sumatra has a half-human/half-animal creature known as the Orang Pendek. The Orang Pendek, whose name means "Short Man," has been rumored to exist as far back as 1295, when Marco Polo reported its existence. Though evidence for the creature's existence has never been officially documented, it has been described as an apelike creature under three feet tall, immensely strong, with short legs, and completely covered with hair. Since 1910 reported sightings have become more common. A Dutch industrialist claimed to see it sitting in a tree above him in 1923. Several dozen unrelated individuals have reported seeing the creature, and many of the descriptions are identical. Recently John Mackinnon, a well-known and highly respected primate researcher, found footprints of what he believes may be the Orang Pendek. It appeared to be a human foot, but the big toes were on the outside. Later, Mackinnon even found old casts of similar footprints in a local museum. Although no substantiated photographs or video documentation exists, many of the local people of Sumatra accept the Orang Pendek's existence to be as real as that of the orangutan.

and access to food and females but also may influence their hormonal activities, suppressing the development of the adult features.

Humans and the orangutan

The orangutan remained hidden from the Western world for many thousands of years. There were, however, a small number of people, indigenous to the islands of Borneo and Sumatra, who knew of their existence long before this last century. These local people lived in the forests in close proximity to the apes. They have long recognized the amazing similarities between humans and orangutans that modern science is just now beginning to understand. From

Orangutans in Myth

The Dayak people of Borneo have lived among orangutans for centuries. Fascinated with the apes, the Dayak have always held them in high regard as near relatives to themselves. The Dayak name for orangutan is *mias*. They developed a number of legends to help explain the *mias*'s existence. In one story, the gods created man and woman and were so pleased with themselves that they had a great feast. They became extremely intoxicated at this feast and forgot exactly how they had achieved their fantastic creation. When they attempted to repeat it, the result was the orangutan. Another story depicts the orangutans as humans who had angered the gods and were covered in long red fur, disfigured, and banished to the forest. Some Dayaks even believe that orangutans are capable of speech but choose not to speak for fear that they will be put to work.

the ancient legends of tribal villagers to the research of today's anthropologists, humans seem to have always been fascinated by the orangutan's "humanness." This fascination, though, has recently begun to cross the line to exploitation, as orangutans are now captured and sold as pets through an illegal black market.

2

Pets and Rehabilitation

LIKE MANY ANIMALS, orangutans have been hunted and exploited by humans. Traditionally, the orangutan has been hunted by local people for food, trophies, and body parts for use as religious artifacts. The number of orangutans taken for these purposes was always small, however, and never threatened the survival of the species as a whole. Today, the situation is quite different. With the advent of modern weaponry and vehicles, orangutan hunting is a far simpler task than ever before. Unlike most other animal poaching, though, the modern hunter's goal is not to drag a carcass out of the forest but instead to capture a live animal.

Exotic pets

Orangutan skulls and trophies still appear in the markets of Kalimantan on occasion. More often, however, infant orangutans are taken from the forest for use in circuses, as performers in roadside tourist attractions, and as pets. Sometimes these captured animals are trained to perform simple servant tasks, but usually they just take on the same role as a household dog or are sometimes treated like human babies, being dressed up in clothes, given a bed, and served at a table with the rest of the family.

The demand for orangutans as pets was strong throughout Asia during the 1980s and early 1990s. By far the largest importer of these pets was Taiwan. During the late 1980s, a television sitcom in that country helped to popularize this

Bringing poachers as much as $15,000 each, baby orangutans are often captured and sold as pets.

unusual practice. According to Ashley Leiman of the Orangutan Foundation International charity, "The demand was attributed to a popular 1986 television programme, *The Naughty Family,* which featured an orangutan named 'Hsiao Li', portrayed as an ideal companion and pet."[2] Leiman states that at least one thousand of the apes were imported by Taiwan during the run of the show. Sold primarily through newspaper ads, the majority of these animals came from Indonesian Borneo.

In Taiwan alone, the imports represented one out of every thirty orangutans left on the planet. An article in the January 1997 issue of *International Wildlife* magazine claimed that there were more orangutans captured and sent off to the pet trade than exist in all the zoos in the world today. In fact, the World Wildlife Fund reported that in 1991 the city of Taipei (capital of Taiwan) had more orangutans per square mile than the native forests of Borneo and Sumatra.

What *The Naughty Family* did not show is what happens when an orangutan grows up. As they reach the age of five or six, they begin to develop incredible strength. An adult male orangutan is said to be as strong as four adult human males. This, combined with the natural limit-testing of an adolescent, makes for an extremely dangerous pet. People are often hurt, and property is often damaged. Eventually, most people end up either having their pet destroyed or sent off to zoos and research facilities. The loss represented by the pets themselves is only part of the picture, however.

Capture and transport

Poachers will only take very young infants for the pet trade, because they are the "cutest" and bring in the highest cash value (a baby orangutan will sell for six to fifteen thousand dollars). Since the infants are in the constant care of their mother, she represents a significant obstacle to the poacher. It is nearly impossible for a person to part a female orangutan from her child, so the mothers are typically shot out of the trees they are sitting in, leaving the infant vulnerable to capture. Due to the orangutan's long inter-birth interval and slow rearing process, the killing of each fertile adult female represents a devastating blow to the wild population.

Once a poacher has captured a baby orangutan, he faces the problem of smuggling his new charge out of the country. It is illegal to ship these animals out of Indonesia or Malaysia, so poachers have become creative about hiding their contraband. They will often stuff the babies into small boxes labeled as art or trinkets. For days, the young orangutans travel in these inhumane conditions without food or water. For this reason, about half of all captured orangutans die before they reach their destination. The ones that are alive upon arrival are typically in poor health. According to the Balikpapan Orangutan

Each year, hundreds of orangutans are imported by nations like Taiwan, which has very loose restrictions against the sale of captive orangutans.

Because they are often smuggled in small boxes without food or water, half of all baby orangutans captured die before reaching their destination.

Society, an organization that raises funds for orangutan rescue efforts, "For every baby that reaches market, three to five other orangutans may have died."[3] They arrive at this number by counting the one live animal to reach its destination, at least one dead traveling companion, and the mothers of each of those animals that were killed. Assuming this figure is accurate, this would mean that during the late 1980s and early 1990s approximately four thousand of the apes were removed from the jungles of Borneo for the pet trade. This number represents about 15 percent of the entire world population of wild orangutans.

Protection

For quite some time it has been illegal to harm, capture, or kill an orangutan. For example, laws protecting them were passed in Indonesia in 1931, in the Malaysian state of Sarawak in 1958, and in Sabah in 1963. While these laws have been on the books for many years, there has been little attempt at enforcing them. Like many other developing nations, Indonesia and Malaysia simply do not have the money or manpower to adequately patrol the forests and airports. As the world focuses its attention on the orangutan, however, countries like Indonesia are put in the spotlight. As a result, efforts at enforcement of antipoaching laws have recently been stepped up. Indonesia imposes a fine of up to fifty thousand dollars for harming or capturing an orangutan. In both Indonesia and Malaysia, more rangers are hired every year to patrol the national parks, and more arrests are widely publicized in the media in an effort to deter poachers.

In 1989 the Taiwanese government was under pressure from the international community and decided to pass its own set of wildlife conservation laws. The new laws required people to register their pets in an attempt to regulate the market. By the end of 1990, only three hundred orangutans were registered, however, despite reports of well over a thousand pets in the country.

While conservation efforts both abroad and in Indonesia and Malaysia have increased, the illegal trade in baby orangutans has definitely slowed down but shows no signs of stopping completely. For example, in 1996 a ranger at a Kalimantan reserve reported that his staff had dealt with

CITES

Transporting orangutans and other animals across national borders is regulated by an international organization known as the Convention on International Trade in Endangered Species (CITES). The organization determines an animal's population status in the wild and then places it in the appropriate category. Animals on their Appendix I list are strictly controlled. No trade across national borders is permitted for any reason. Animals on lower appendixes (II and III) are allowed to be traded, but the trade is monitored and under strict control. The orangutan is on Appendix I, so it is officially protected in most countries. However, joining CITES and adhering to its rulings is strictly voluntary. Taiwan is not a member of CITES and is not required to adhere to its general policies. As a result, few efforts were made to curb the extensive orangutan import business in that country. Poachers that illegally trapped the animals in Malaysia and Indonesia were allowed to freely sell their wares on the open market in Taiwan. Today, the international community is pressuring Taiwan to join CITES, but the country has yet to accede.

seven cases of baby orangutan smuggling in a period of a few weeks. Furthermore, rescuing an orphaned orangutan from its captors is just the beginning of a long, difficult, and expensive process.

Orangutan rehabilitation

In the past one of the biggest problems facing the Indonesian and Malaysian governments was finding appropriate homes for all of the orphaned animals that the governments confiscated. As babies, the orphaned orangutans would never survive on their own if returned to the wild. Likewise, zoos lacked room for them all, and the governments had no suitable facilities. The answer to this problem had its origins in a facility created in the 1960s by a woman named Barbara Harrisson.

In 1958 local officials gave Harrisson's husband, who was the curator of the Sarawak Museum, a confiscated orangutan infant in need of care. Barbara Harrisson took over the responsibility of caring for the infant, and she proceeded to raise it as a human mother would raise a child. Over the years, the Harrissons were given several more orangutans that had been kept as pets and continued to raise them in this fashion. Eventually Barbara Harrisson journeyed out into the nearby forest in an effort to observe how wild orangutans cared for their own young. Harrisson realized that her methods were inappropriate and would never result in animals that could live in the wild. Her first seven charges had to be sent off to zoos when they matured because they had spent too many of their formative years in the company of humans. They could never be successfully returned to the jungle.

The Harrissons continued to take in a never-ending stream of wayward orphans. Barbara Harrisson then began utilizing what she had observed in the forest, trying to teach the young orangutans the skills they would need to live an independent life in the wild. In the process, she formulated what would become the basis for modern methods of orangutan rehabilitation. The first step in the process was education to semiwilderness. This involved exposing

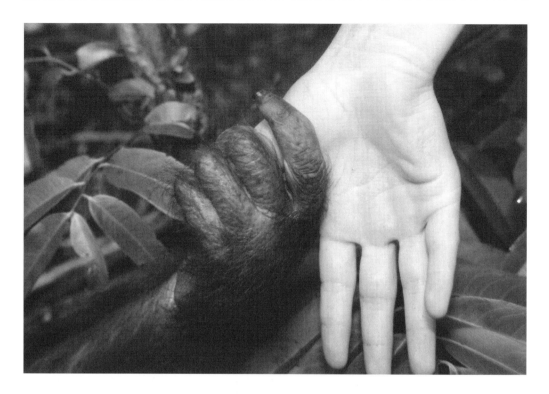

the human-imprinted babies to the jungle, where they could climb trees, gather food, make nests, and interact with other orangutans. The next step was to transfer them full time to a jungle enclosure. The young orangutans would live in a section of forest that had been sealed off while they honed their survival skills, but they could still rely on reserve food and protection from their human bene-factors. The last step was to release them altogether. Harrisson would observe them for a period after release to see how they were adapting. Unfortunately, all her attempts ended in failure, as the only area she had to release them in did not contain any of the proper fruit trees to support orangutans. The orangutans involved in these efforts either died or were shipped off to zoos.

Harrisson's attempts and innovations, however, did inspire the Malaysian government to establish a new rehabilitation and release site in 1964. It was located farther north in Borneo, near Sepilok, in a pristine ten-thousand-acre forest already populated with orangutans. This facility was

Exposing human-imprinted babies to the jungle is a vital step in preparing them for release back into the wild.

A Controversial Rehabilitation Worker

In October 1990 ten young orangutans were confiscated in Taiwan. The Taiwanese government wanted to send them back to Borneo to be rehabilitated and returned to the wild. Amidst much attention from the news media, Birute Galdikas prepared to receive the apes at her rehabilitation center, Camp Leakey. However, she had recently begun to fall out of favor with the Indonesian government. As a result, the orangutans were detained in Jakarta (Indonesia's capital) for nearly a year. Galdikas protested and was even accused of masterminding an attempt to break them out of their holding station. The government never did give the apes to Galdikas. Instead, most of them were sent to the Wanariset Orangutan Rehabilitation Center in eastern Kalimantan.

Often at odds with officials, Birute Galdikas has nevertheless done a great deal of work to protect the orangutan.

called the Sabah Orangutan Rehabilitation Center. Begun by a man named Stanley de Silva, it successfully released a number of formerly captive orangutans to the wild.

The rehabilitation concept then spread to Sumatra. In 1971 a Dutch primatologist named Herman Rijksen established a new rehabilitation center in an area known as Ketambe, located in what would later become the Gunung Leuser National Park. At first, Rijksen only provided the animals with basic medical care and then sent them out into the forest. Eventually, however, he began to develop techniques to educate the orangutans about the homes to which they would one day return. His techniques were largely based on Harrisson's work. Rijksen was not the only one working on orangutan rehabilitation, though. During the same year, one of the most famous—and most controversial—centers opened. Called Camp Leakey, the research center in Kalimantan's Tanjung Puting Forest was established by Birute Galdikas. The methods she used there demonstrated a driving passion to protect the orangutans and eventually brought worldwide attention to their plight. In 1973 another facility opened on the other side of the Gunung Leuser National Park in Sumatra.

It was just a little more than a decade later that the large boom in the orangutan pet trade spawned the creation of several more rehabilitation sites, including ones in Tanjung Harrapan and Wanariset. Rehabilitation centers were popping up all over Indonesia and Malaysia, but each had its own methods. As orangutan rehabilitation has become more widely practiced, several issues regarding rehabilitation methods have become controversial topics in the primate research community. Practices that were once commonplace have suddenly been brought into question.

Intervention vs. interaction

In the early days of rehabilitation, the orphans were usually kept in the homes of the rehabbers, or workers. In an attempt to keep them healthy and happy, the orangutans would be allowed to cling to a human surrogate mother for as long as they desired. Workers found it hard not to coddle the infants, as many of the babies were neurotic and prone to withdrawal or tantrums. This practice came under scrutiny when people began realizing that it stripped the orangutans of their "wildness" and prevented their successful return to the forest. According to Terry Maple, a well-known primate researcher and the director of Zoo Atlanta, one of the major problems with releasing formerly captive apes back into the wild is the difficulty in training a human-dependent, ground-adapted, socialized animal to be arboreal and afraid of people.

In addition to being dependent on humans, orangutans raised in excessively close contact with people can be severely maladjusted to life in the forest. Some demonstrate a fear of heights and, once returned to the wild, refuse to climb trees since they have never done it before. This causes obvious complications because the apes' food supply grows in trees. An even more serious problem for the newly released captives is that they will also seek out humans for companionship and food. These orangutans will sometimes venture into nearby villages, where they are often unwelcome and are sometimes shot. Another complication, Maple points out, is the presence of ecotourist volunteers who assist in the rehab process. These untrained individuals are usually there to "cuddle" with the babies, and since they are paying large sums of money to be there, they usually get their wish. This constant influx of tourists undermines the rehab facilities' attempts to reduce the apes' dependence on humans.

An untrained volunteer cuddles a baby orangutan. Some experts feel that this type of behavior on the part of humans is harmful to the orangutan.

While most rehabbers agree on the need to separate the soon-to-be-released orangutans from humans, Birute Galdikas is still a strong proponent of the "coddling" method. Her methods have recently become the topic of considerable controversy. Galdikas continues to play foster mother to a large number of orangutans. She lets them cling to her and sleep with her. She strongly believes that each orangutan should decide for itself when, or if, it will return to the wild. Her facility, Camp Leakey, still has a number of what Galdikas calls "bicultural residents"—orangutans who are equally comfortable in the wild and around people. According to Galdikas, "Camp Leakey is a place where humans interface with the

Orangutan Abuse

Many of the young orangutans that are confiscated and brought into rehabilitation centers come from unpleasant or even abusive situations. Some of them arrive having spent their entire childhoods in cages hardly big enough for them to turn around in. Some were chained up and unable to move at all. One orangutan was even reported to have been confined to the empty engine space of a truck for several years, being fed through a hole in the hood. Another had accompanied her "father" to local taverns every night and arrived at the facility an alcoholic. Just as with humans, this type of abuse can have an extremely detrimental effect on the apes' future social and physical development. Unfortunately, many of the more severely abused orangutans never become successfully rehabilitated back to the forest.

wild, and if some orangutans are at ease at this interface and also at ease in the wilderness, they're successful rehabilitants."[4]

Where to call home?

Regardless of the methods used to rehabilitate an orangutan, the problem of where it should be released arises. Until recently, most rehab facilities were set up to release their charges into habitats currently occupied by wild orangutans. Such areas were guaranteed to have suitable habitats for the apes, including the proper food sources. However, there are inherent problems associated with this practice. Herman Rijksen was one of the first to address these problems. As he points out, "If orangutans are already in an area where you release some, you risk overloading the carrying capacity [of that area]."[5] By adding a continuous flow of outside orangutans, the ecosystem and its resources are pushed beyond their capacity. Something must give, and eventually the area's orangutan population will begin to thin itself. Obviously, this defeats the whole purpose of rehabilitation.

The other problem with releasing orangutans into a currently inhabited area is the risk of spreading disease. Because of their genetic similarity to humans, orangutans are able to contract a wide variety of diseases from their owners. In Taiwan and Indonesia, for example, hepatitis and tuberculosis are common. After spending a number of years living in close contact with humans, whether as pets or as performers, many orangutans arrive at the rehabilitation facilities with a variety of communicable diseases. Releasing these animals into an established population of wild apes is extremely risky. A potentially deadly disease could be released into the environment and devastate the local orangutan population.

Birute Galdikas, however, does not agree with this theory. She continues to release orangutans into areas already populated by orangutans, arguing that these protected national parks are the only places where her rehabilitants will be safe from poachers. She claims that this is a safe prac-

Visitors play with an orangutan at Camp Leakey. The camp is in danger of losing its permits for refusing to comply with government regulations.

tice, citing as proof the fact that "there haven't been any epidemics or wild orangutans dropping dead."[6] Galdikas's position is currently at odds with the official stance of the International Union for the Conservation of Nature and Natural Resources that rehabilitants do pose a serious threat to wild orangutans.

While the threat of epidemic may continue to be argued, the fact remains that previously captive animals do arrive at rehabilitation sites infected with diseases. A relatively new facility, the Wanariset Orangutan Reintroduction Center, reports that 70 percent of its initial 114 orangutans were carriers (symptomatic or asymptomatic) for some type of disease or parasite. Ashley Leiman, a representative of the Orangutan Foundation International, reports that out of a group of 30 incoming orangutans inspected by her organization, all were riddled with parasites; 11 were infected with hepatitis B and 4 had tuberculosis.

The sixth congress of the International Primatological Society recently condemned the reintroduction of orangutans into previously populated areas. Official statements such as this have led the Indonesian government to pass laws making it illegal to release formerly captive orangutans into areas populated by wild apes. Galdikas has refused to comply, and as a result, Camp Leakey is currently in danger of losing its government permits to work with captive orangutans.

Rehabilitation methods

Regardless of the controversies surrounding the release of former captives, the rehabilitation process is often the same. Many important steps are involved in the rehabilitation of a pet orangutan. The first—and perhaps most important—is simply confiscating the animal from its unsafe environment. Confiscation is rarely an easy task, though. Due to corruption in the Indonesian government, wealthy orangutan owners—who may view owning a red ape as a status symbol—are often above the law. In other cases, people simply become very attached to their pets, and they cannot bear the thought of parting with them.

People have to be slowly and delicately convinced that their pets would be better off in the wild. In many cases, law enforcement officials must be called in to help forcibly remove the animals.

Quarantine

All orangutans that come into rehabilitation facilities are treated as if they may be carrying any number of deadly diseases. In addition to carrying various diseases and parasites, some of the animals that come in have been obviously mistreated.

Once former pets arrive at an authorized rehabilitation facility, they are placed in quarantine cages. First, they are fingerprinted and have their pictures taken. This helps staff members identify the orangutans during both rehabilitation and postrelease research. Next, the orangutans are put through a full battery of tests and procedures to determine their health. Much like a complete physical for humans, blood is drawn and the orangutans' body temperature, blood pressure, pulse, and breathing rate are all checked. Hair and nail samples are also taken for use in DNA tests.

New arrivals are typically left in these quarantine cages—where they can see other infants but cannot touch them—for a period of thirty days. The animals are vaccinated against a variety of human diseases such as polio, malaria, encephalitis, hepatitis, and tuberculosis. The orangutans are also treated for parasites such as tapeworms and lice, which plague the vast majority of new arrivals. Often the orangutans are malnourished, either from neglect or from being fed an inappropriate diet. If the animals are found to have a communicable disease, they are treated and held for a much longer period. Since they often arrive seriously ill, it is not uncommon for a number of new arrivals to die while in quarantine. Once given a clean bill of health, the orangutans are placed in a communal cage with apes of similar ages.

To prevent the spread of diseases to wild populations, orangutans are immediately quarantined when they arrive at rehabilitation centers.

Social rehabilitation is considered the first step to an orangutan's eventual return to the wild.

Social rehabilitation

At this point, the actual rehabilitation—teaching the animal how to survive in the wild—begins. The rehabbers try to intervene in ways that will stimulate natural behaviors and facilitate their charges' return to the wild. Herman Rijksen has identified two primary stages in successful rehabilitation. The first is social rehabilitation. This has been described as a process "in which orangutans develop positive social contacts with their peers and with wild orangutans."[7] While an orangutan spends most of its life in solitude, the infrequent encounters it has with others of its kind are still an integral part of its life in the wild. Females need to know how to attract a mate, for example, or participate in short-term associations with other females. Similarly, males need to know the finer points of courtship if they ever hope to reproduce. The male also has the added responsibility of learning how to defend himself and his territory from would-be invaders.

The social rehabilitation is made more complicated by the fact that many captive apes have no memory of having seen another of their own kind; thus, they do not know how to interact appropriately with other orangutans. Initial socialization is accomplished by placing the apes in communal nurseries, where they learn to seek comfort and companionship from other orangutans rather than from humans. They also gain the opportunity to learn social skills from the older members of the group. By forming these bonds, they will be prepared to interact with each other after they are reintroduced into the wild.

Ecological rehabilitation

Feeding platforms are used to gradually reduce orangutans' contact with humans and to help them adjust to life in the jungle.

The second stage referred to by Rijksen is ecological rehabilitation, which consists of teaching the apes how to live in a forest. British orangutan researcher Isabelle Lardeux-Gilloux refers to this as the important step whereby "orangutans develop maintenance [skills] on their own and are no longer dependent on [humans] for food."[8] Most

of these orangutans have not seen a tree or vine-ripened fruit since they were just a few weeks old. To familiarize them with their new home, the orangutans are taken out to the forest, where they are placed in large communal cages that hold former captives of varying ages. First, the orangutans must become desensitized to this environment, which offers many sounds, smells, and sights that are unfamiliar and frightening to the young apes. Once the animals seem comfortable in their new surroundings, the cage doors are left open during the day and closed only at night. At this point, the orangutans can begin to explore their new environment.

There is much to learn. Captive orangutans have, for example, no concept of how to forage for food or build nests. Because orangutans spend the majority of their lives—and find most of their food—in trees, teaching the infants to be competent climbers is an important first step. The orangutans are usually taken out each day and are encouraged to climb vines or short trees. Studies have shown that youngsters provided with ropes in their nursery cages typically did better at tree climbing in the wild. Once they have overcome their fear and mastered their coordination, they begin learning how to forage for their own food.

Feeding platforms are built in the trees near the apes' sleeping cages. The young orangutans quickly learn to climb up to the platforms for treats. However, the treats soon become less interesting than the plethora of fruits around them. Orangutans depend heavily on an extremely diverse group of foods for survival. By placing only one consistent type of fruit on the platform each day, the apes are encouraged to look for other fruits elsewhere. The infants will follow the older members of the group and learn from them how to find and open a large number of different fruits. In this way, they are encouraged to become independent from the platform and thus from any human assistance. The slower learners, though, will still have the platform treats to rely on so they do not go hungry.

At night the younger orangutans are provided with nesting material in their cages; by watching the older animals, they learn to create nests of their own. Eventually the cages are left open at night, as well as during the day, and the orangutans are encouraged to go out and make nests in the trees. Since they receive no food in the cage, they tend not to return to it anymore; instead, they will start to move farther and farther out on their own. Gradually, less food is provided at the feeding station, and there is only minimal, if any, human contact permitted at these sites.

Each orangutan sets its own schedule for leaving the release area. Studies have shown that during the fruit season, many orangutans will permanently leave the area in as little as two weeks. During the dry season, however, it may take as long as three months before the former captives move on. Once they have left the area, only a few individuals return for infrequent visits.

Rehabilitation hurdles

Not every former captive can be rehabilitated, however. An orangutan's success at rehabilitation can often be predicted by its age. Apes that arrive when they are older tend to be set in their ways and are often unable to grasp the rudiments of social interaction. A common cause of failure during the first stage of rehabilitation is a neurosis developed in captivity. Such psychological problems occur as a result of being raised out of the orangutan's natural element. All former captives are orphans that were violently removed from their mothers and their natural surroundings, but some orangutans adapt better to these extremely traumatic early-life circumstances than others. The less fortunate ones develop odd behaviors and extreme anxiety in uncomfortable situations, which are often expressed in the form of rocking, tantrums, regurgitation and reingestion, finger sucking, and aggressive displays. The inability to deal with new situations will hinder these unfortunate individuals in each stage of rehabilitation.

This orangutan is sucking its fingers, a sign that it is having problems with rehabilitation.

Another common problem among rehab orangutans is "flat feet syndrome." Because they were removed from the forest early in life, their grips are often poorly developed. Youngsters in the wild spend every moment of their first few months tightly gripped to their mothers' fur. This activity helps orangutans develop strength in their grips, which former pets often lack. The severity of this deficiency will often determine whether an animal can survive on its own in the forest. Orangutans that are unable to adapt to the forest environment will spend the rest of their lives either at rehabilitation facilities or in zoos.

Home at last

Once the apes are successfully returned to the wild, they can begin their new lives as wild orangutans. An enormous amount of time, energy, and money goes into rehabilitating these orangutans, and some critics have even questioned the usefulness of such establishments. Ashley Leiman fears that the recent successes of these centers may "distract attention from the need to conserve more protected areas."[9]

Whatever the long-term effects might be, these facilities certainly provide a number of short-term benefits. Perhaps the most important benefit is that they provide a place for authorities to send confiscated animals. Without the presence of these facilities, law enforcement officials would never go to the trouble of removing the orangutans from their ill-equipped owners. Moreover, such facilities provide a far superior quality of life than these apes would experience in captivity. In the forest they can act like orangutans, and they will be free to live out the duration of their lives. In captivity, however, they usually only last until age six or seven, at which time they are either euthanized or are sent to research facilities where they can become subjects in medical experiments. Zoos simply do not have enough room to take in the vast number of unwanted apes coming out of Southeast Asia.

Aside from benefitting rescued orangutans, the rehabilitation facilities fulfill other vital functions. Many of them are responsible for preserving small regions of habitat for release sites. In addition, they provide benefits to the local people. Most rehab facilities are actively engaged in outreach education. Local residents are brought to the sites and are taught about the rehabilitation process, which helps them to understand the importance of preserving the species for the future. Finally, the release sites also provide the perfect opportunity for researchers to conduct behavioral studies on wild orangutans.

Overall, these rehabilitation centers appear to be a great boon to the orangutan species. However, their very existence signals that poaching continues to threaten wild populations. Efforts are being made by the Indonesian and Malaysian governments to curb these activities, but as long as there is a price on their heads, baby orangutans will never be completely safe from poachers.

3

Habitat Loss

WHILE POACHING AND the illegal animal trade pose serious threats to the future of the orangutan, they pale in comparison to the larger problem of habitat loss. The single most significant problem faced by all endangered plants and animals on the earth is that they are simply running out of places to live. There is only a finite amount of space and resources on the planet. When the population of one species grows and takes up more of those resources, another species loses out and pays the consequence: a thinning out of its population.

The human population has grown enormously over the last few centuries. As a result, humans have usurped an incredible amount of the world's resources. Researchers who study population trends estimate that by the end of this century 6 billion people will inhabit the earth; by the year 2040, that number will have doubled. This expansion has pushed many other plant and animal species to the brink of extinction.

Asian habitat

A vision of what is to come can already be seen throughout Asia, which has the planet's greatest human population density. For example, at the beginning of the twentieth century Indonesia's human population was 10 million. Today, it stands at approximately 200 million. With this twentyfold increase in population has come an enormous demand for new living space and for more land where crops can be grown to feed hungry mouths.

43

In 1978 Herman Rijksen published a study about orangutan populations and determined that, as a result of habitat destruction, the red ape's habitat had been reduced by 20 to 30 percent since the 1930s. At the time, this was a startling and even frightening revelation. What researchers and the world could not know, however, was that over the next twenty years an additional 50 to 60 percent of that habitat would be lost. According to a press release from the World Wildlife Fund, "Eighty percent of the orangutan's original habitat has been destroyed."[10] A number of factors have led to this destruction. Chief among them are the increased agricultural demands of so many people, but the sheer number of trees that have been removed for commercial uses is also a factor.

The dramatic increase of Indonesia's population in recent decades has drastically reduced the amount of jungle where orangutans can live.

Logging

It is fairly common for developing nations to rely on some sort of commercial timber industry as an important part of their economy. Indonesia is no exception. Thirty-five years ago, massive clear-cutting began throughout the forests of Indonesia. The industry had just taken off, and no regulations were in place to control the amount or type of logging conducted. Today, the government claims to understand the need to manage its timber resources wisely. However, much of the damage has already been done. According to recent studies, approximately 40 percent of Indonesia's forests have already been cleared; the equivalent of fifty acres per minute continues to be logged every day.

Logging is another threat to the orangutan's habitat.

A necessary industry?

The Indonesian government purports to understand the long-term risks of deforestation, including its devastating effect on the lives of the country's most charismatic endangered primate: the orangutan. However, logging practices, while controlled to some degree, still continue. The timber industry is of utmost importance to Indonesia; it is the country's third-largest export (after oil and textiles). In 1996 wood products accounted for $5.5 billion in exports while paper and pulp products contributed another $1.4 billion. Today, the forestry industry directly employs 3.7 million people. Forestry also indirectly supports another 11 million Indonesians through jobs in the paper and timber product industries, such as shipping, packaging, and manufacturing companies.

The complete elimination of this industry would cripple the economies of both Indonesia and Malaysia. For example, the taxes paid by logging companies are the primary sources of revenue for the Malaysian state of Sabah. Even faraway nations have a stake in the region's forest industry. Japan has a small timber supply and must import more

Indonesia's Rain Forest Diversity

Indonesia is considered to be one of the most biologically diverse regions on the earth. As the habitat shared by orangutans and countless other species continues to be decimated, conservationists fear that this amazing diversity may be lost forever. Biologists estimate that Indonesia is home to 10 percent of the world's entire tropical rain forest habitat and 17 percent of the world's flora and fauna species. In addition, the country has more animals listed on the IUCN's endangered species list than any other nation—128 mammals and 104 birds. In fact, there are 18,381 species of bird that exist in Indonesia and nowhere else. Plant researchers have found that just ten hectares of Bornean rain forest contain 700 different species of tree, equal to the total number of tree species found throughout all of North America. If these rain forests are allowed to disappear, the orangutan will be just one of many plant and animal species that will fade from the earth forever.

Indonesia is estimated to be the home of 10 percent of the world's rain forest habitat.

than 70 percent of the wood used there. Indonesia has an annual $2 billion debt to Japan, and it relies on timber exports to make yearly payments on that debt.

Since Malaysia and Indonesia cannot afford to stop logging altogether, they have made some attempts to control it. Unfortunately, many of the rules and regulations they have put into place are ineffective. These nations simply do not have adequate financial resources to enforce all of the laws that they create. Furthermore, according to recent reports, many of the Japanese-owned logging corporations in Sabah and Sarawak have been allowed to break certain rules because the Malaysian government fears that Japan may pull its companies out of Malaysia. Consequently, authorities overlook the fact that many of these large corporations fail to practice required safe-harvesting techniques or to replant the regions they have deforested. In addition to the Japanese corporations, the wealthy and powerful owners of a number of other timber companies are well connected in the Indonesian and Malaysian governments. These "timber barons" often operate as if they are above the law. In return for favors and timber concessions, they offer financial incentives to officials in the Indonesian and Malaysian governments. Logging, however, is only part of the picture when it comes to destruction of the orangutan's habitat.

Agriculture

The human populations on Borneo and Sumatra have been steadily expanding over the last few decades, and Indonesia is having trouble finding room for all of its people. Development and subsequent human relocations can also be problems. In 1979, for example, 1 million people were relocated to Borneo from overcrowded conditions on the island of Java. In the last twenty years, this transplanted population has continued to grow. As the population on these islands surges, new ways to feed the masses must be found; thus, the amount of land devoted to agriculture must expand.

Land resources are vast but still finite. As a result, the same soil that nourishes the orangutan's rain forest home is now needed to grow crops for humans. For many centuries, local people used a method of farming known as slash and burn. This involved burning an area of forest to the ground in order to clear it for planting. All the nutrients of the burned forest were deposited in the soil, which made a perfect environment for the crops to grow. Ironically, because

Erosion

Erosion can be a devastating side effect of selective logging. The ground beneath a rain forest is usually composed of nutrient-poor clay soil. What makes it rich is the constant carpet of decaying leaves, fruits, branches, and dead animals. Rain is filtered down to the ground through a dense canopy of foliage. The process of decay deposits nutrients into the soil; these nutrients are then taken up by the growing trees and foliage. To make use of these nutrients, the roots must grow shallow. Even when only the largest trees are removed from the rain forest, huge gaps are created in the canopy. As a result, the daily downpour of rain can now reach the ground uninhibited and wash away all of the life-sustaining nutrients, leaving the soil barren. The trees that remain will usually die along with the animals that depend on them.

Even if only a few trees are removed, the resulting erosion may lead to the eventual destruction of large areas of rain forest.

it is the cycle of growth in the living forest itself that supplies needed nutrients, cleared land cannot be farmed indefinitely. Indigenous people would work these lands until the nutrients had been exhausted. They would then move on to another area, allowing the forest to regenerate on the abandoned fields. In the past, when there were just isolated tribes of people on these islands, this method worked well because the small patches of burned rain forest had time to recover. As the amount of food needed by the expanding local population has continued to multiply, more and more forest is giving way to farmland. Because the cycle of slash-and-burn farming accelerates with each passing year, it may not be long before there is no forest left for orangutans or for humans. Thus, the problem that must be addressed is how to balance the needs of both orangutans and humans.

Land-use categories

Proper management of the forests will be a critical factor in long-term preservation of orangutan habitat. Indonesia's government has gone on record a number of times stating that it is committed to preserving rain forest habitats as well as orangutans and all other life-forms dwelling within them. To this end, it has created a land-use system to ensure that certain patches of forest are completely protected from human activity. Under this system, a high level of protection is afforded to national parks and wildlife refuges. These areas make up about 16 percent of all remaining forestland and 9 percent of Indonesia's entire land base. These parks are often open to the public for camping and wildlife viewing, as well as a number of other uses, but no development is permitted within the boundaries of a designated park.

The next category recognized by the Indonesian government is "protected forest." These areas have unique environmental and hydrological characteristics that make them indispensable to the habitat and the local human populations. A region of protected forest is completely closed to commercial and even recreational uses. The closed zones account for approximately 27 percent of Indonesia's total forest area.

In "limited-production forests," selective timber harvesting is permitted as long as certain environmental concerns are addressed. A number of regulations concerning safe timber-harvesting practices must be adhered to, including ones about extraction limits and replanting requirements.

New Ways of Logging

While the timber industry will probably be around for quite some time, efforts have been made to reduce the impact of logging practices. Selective logging—the removal of only a small, specified percentage of the trees in a given area—has been a policy for some time. However, the methods used to remove these trees can cause immeasurable damage to all the surrounding trees. A new government regulation requires that vines attached to the target tree be cut before the tree is felled. This prevents the large tree from tearing down all of the smaller trees that are connected to it by vines. Another consideration is "directional felling." This method would protect neighboring trees by carefully cutting the target tree so that it falls in a direction that will do the least damage to the surrounding foliage. Also, skid rails are laid in the ground to allow smooth removal of trees from the area. Loggers are required to use these skid rails for all extractions and to bring all of the trees to one central location where they can be loaded onto a truck. In the past, massive trucks were driven into the center of the forest, leaving paths of destruction in their wake. All these efforts should help to reduce the damage caused by timber harvesting.

Directional felling is one logging method used to reduce the damage done to the rain forest.

Limited-production forests make up another 27 percent of the remaining wild lands.

The final official category is "regular-production forests." Here, large-scale production of timber, rattan, saps, and other forest products is permitted under government-regulated guidelines. These guidelines limit the number of plant and animal species that can be disturbed in any one area. According to the Indonesian government, regular-production forests make up about another 30 percent of the forests. However, the Environmental Investigation Agency, an independent group dedicated to exposing environmental cover-ups and disseminating information, reports that this is a gross underestimation. The agency claims that this category of forest makes up 45 percent of the nation's total forested area.

In addition, 70 million acres of nontropical forestland (i.e., shrubs, grasslands, and swamps) have been earmarked as "conversion areas." This means that, due to a low level of biodiversity and commercial harvest potential, these lands will be converted to agricultural uses, timber plantations, or human resettlement sites. By sacrificing these areas to development, the government hopes to safeguard the tropical forests.

Further complications

Not everyone is convinced that logging and orangutans are incompatible, though. Many of Indonesia's governmental regulations concentrate on limiting the number of trees that are removed from any given patch of forest. They also mandate that timber companies plant new trees to replace the ones that are removed. This concept of "light logging" is based on the idea that it is less damaging to the environment to remove small numbers of trees from a larger patch than to clear-cut a smaller patch. In theory, the orangutans would be able to move to an area where logging was not presently going on; then, as the loggers caught up with them, the orangutans could cycle to a new area, eventually ending up in their original territory. It is hoped that light logging will be less damaging to the

It is hoped that light logging will be less destructive to rain forests than the methods currently used (pictured).

ecosystem as a whole and, when coupled with replanting efforts, will allow the habitat time to regenerate.

While this plan may be theoretically sound, some critics disagree with its underlying assumptions. One problem pointed out by a report from the International Union for the Conservation of Nature and Natural Resources, for example, is that even when timber companies adhere to the guidelines governing the number of trees they can harvest, the methods they use are often more destructive than the actual timber harvesting itself. Removing large trees requires the assistance of large machinery. To get that machinery into the area, wide roads are cut through the center of the rain forest. The trees that are knocked down during the road-building process are not counted in the official harvest tally, however, because they are never removed and processed. Not only do these roads take out many trees, they also form effective barriers for many rain forest creatures, effectively cutting them off from part of their habitat.

Another concern involves the way in which the trees are cut down. The larger trees are the target of most timber companies, but when a 150-foot tree falls, it usually takes out a number of smaller trees and shrubs on the way down. Again, the timber companies are not held accountable for the trees that are damaged in this way. Often, each tree removed represents ten or more trees that have been damaged or completely destroyed during the harvesting process.

Large-scale protection

According to biologists, losing raw acreage of rain forest is only half the problem for many animals, including orangutans. Habitat fragmentation is just as serious a threat. The only real way to protect plants and animals, these scientists contend, is to protect complete ecosystems. The interconnected nature of the rain forest ecosystem means that even a small disturbance in one area can have an enormous impact on the whole forest. One of the problems with most current timber-harvesting methods is that they create isolated pockets, or islands, of habitat that are cut off from the rest of the ecosystem. According to Herman Rijksen, "Many of the remaining orangutans are in fragments of forest far too small to support the population."[11]

In the case of the orangutan, this problem is often referred to when discussing genetics. When a small group of orangutans is cut off from any contact with other groups, it will begin inbreeding. This prevents the opportunity for genetic exchange, which, on a long-term basis, can leave the small group ill-equipped to cope with a changing environment. Inbreeding can also lead to serious health problems and may eventually cause the extinction of that local population.

 Genetic Exchange

The ways in which the orangutan's habitat is being reduced will not only affect the number of animals left in the forest but also their ability to adapt and survive. Many orangutans now live in small isolated pockets of rain forest that are cut off from other local subpopulations. One of the most important components to the longevity of any species is the ability to exchange and combine genetic material. This is how the process of evolution functions. Random mutations from these genetic combinations can lead to unusual new traits in plants and animals. If the new traits leave an organism poorly suited for the environment it lives in, it will probably not live long enough to reproduce and pass on those traits. If the adaptation is useful, it may give a plant or animal a competitive edge, providing it with a longer and more robust life. This typically transfers to higher rates of reproduction, which allows more of the "successful" DNA to be passed on. If the orangutan is to survive as a species, it must be able to mix and breed with as many others of its kind as possible. This, of course, requires the presence of large, unbroken stretches of rain forest habitat.

The ideal solution to this problem would be to leave entire ecosystems intact. This is clearly not possible in all areas of Indonesia and Malaysia, but there are alternatives. The creation of biological corridors is one option. This involves the establishment of forested pathways between the habitat pockets. By setting aside these relatively narrow strips of land—and replanting them or preventing initial development—animals, including orangutans, can still move from one area to another. In this way, the apes can utilize different food sources and young males can migrate out of the range where they were born and mate with females that are less likely to be close relatives.

The fires of Borneo

Agriculture and the timber industry are not the only threats to the orangutan's habitat. Since the middle of 1997, the forests of Borneo have been continuously ravaged by wildfires. After burning for well over a year, the fires show no signs of slowing. Juwono Sudarsono, Indonesia's former environment minister, claims that these cataclysmic fires are the result of both the unusual weather conditions caused by El Niño and the irresponsible practice of slash-and-burn farming. Sudarsono claims that "about 50 percent of the situation has been caused by human behavior."[12] Indonesia passed laws against slash-and-burn farming in 1995, but timber companies continue to break these regulations on a regular basis. The sheer number of agricultural fires set each year on Borneo is a hazard to the surrounding forests, even during normal weather conditions. According to scientists, however, "blame for the drought and fires can be partly attributed to the El Niño weather phenomenon, which has caused freak weather patterns on both sides of the Pacific Ocean."[13] These unusual weather conditions had left Borneo in one of the worst droughts in its history. The large coastal stretch of southeastern Borneo, where many of these fires are raging, had received less than twelve inches of rainfall in a twelve-month period between 1997 and 1998. The normal rainfall for that area is roughly ten times that amount, so the island has been a tinderbox for some time.

Nowhere to run

These fires have devastated the landscape. In just a five-month period, from January to May 1998, approximately 1.2 million acres of forest were destroyed, including half of the entire Kutai National Park. As these fires raze large sections of orangutan habitat, the animals are forced to flee. Many fail to make it out, either dying of smoke inhalation or simply getting trapped in the fire.

The orangutans that survive the fires face other serious problems. The fires often push them into inappropriate habitat. The real tragedy strikes when orangutans flee out of the forest and into human villages. The expression "out of the frying pan and into the fire," applies quite well, but in reverse. With their homes and sources of food burnt to the ground, the orangutans arrive in the villages quite hungry and usually go straight for the farmers' crops. According to Elizabeth Kemp, species information officer for the World Wildlife Fund, "Villagers, who are suffering from famine and serious respiratory ailments [as a result of the fires], are so desperate that they are killing the orangutans who are fleeing the forests and foraging in their fields and gardens. As [the villagers'] suffering increases, so does their resentment of animals which they would not normally kill."[14] In addition, poachers have been killing females and collecting their babies with renewed vigor. According to Willie Smits, director of the Wanariset Orangutan Reintroduction Center (WORC), during the summer of 1997 only 13 apes near the center's home region of Balikpapan were killed in the fires, but "at least 120 orangutans have been tortured or killed by residents."[15]

Not all local people are out to kill the orangutans. Some recognize their plight and even attempt to help them by leaving out food or calling the forestry department to come to their aid. The staff of the WORC and Indonesia's Ministry of Forestry have been working together to help care for the displaced animals. They travel to villages where orangutans have been sighted and capture the animals for transport. The WORC has given up some of its rehabilitation space to house these unfortunate refugees from the

The Dayaks

As the human population grows and development continues to progress at an unprecedented rate, nature becomes unbalanced. However, animals and plants are not the only casualties of progress. Many native cultures throughout the world are also endangered. Indigenous people, whose ancestors have lived by certain beliefs and practices for thousands of years, are forced to either give up their traditional ways or perish. For centuries, Borneo has been home to the Dayak people. This collective term refers to a number of different subcultures, all of which are connected by their basic language and traditions.

Dayaks are known for the importance they place on being at peace with the world around them. Traditionally, they farmed the land (through methods of slash and burn) and harvested rubber, resin, fruits, and lumber from the trees. However, they were always keenly aware of the ecological balance in the forest and would never take enough plants or animals to upset that balance. Today, the Dayaks are disappearing. Although they were given certain territorial and political rights by the Indonesian government, these rights are often disregarded by the same government that granted them. Logging and agricultural companies take Dayak land for development while officials look the other way. The Dayaks are also sorely underrepresented in the Indonesian legislature. Many Dayaks have chosen to assimilate into Western culture in order to get an education or learn trades that will help them make enough money to survive. While the individuals who make that choice may live on, it would seem that the culture of their ancestors may not.

fires. As of October 1998, the center had 175 orangutan residents, although it is only designed to hold 150. Unfortunately, the rescue efforts are not always successful. Smits described one day when he was just a little too late: "Thirty minutes before, in a small village, another four to five year old orangutan was killed by the village people when it ran out of the burning forest into a villager's tree."[16]

The outlook

These fires are having an effect not only on the forest animals but also on the local people. The humans in the area are suffering from famine and severe water shortages. This has led to a variety of health problems. Crops and property are being completely destroyed, many schools and businesses are being forced to close, and tourism has come to a standstill. These problems will be devastating to Indonesia's economy. According to Thomas Fuller of the *International Herald Tribune,* the fires will set the region's economy back about $6 billion. These economic setbacks, in turn, will affect efforts to protect orangutans; typically, when a nation experiences financial crises, issues such as forest management and conservation tend to become lower priorities.

Many groups are fighting valiantly to combat the fires. According to Smits, the WORC "had one hundred people working day and night for nine months, patrolling and putting out fires wherever they could."[17] Despite their tireless efforts, only twenty of the thirty-five hundred hectares of one branch of their research site remain. As weather conditions return to normal, perhaps nature will step in and douse the fires. Until then, both the orangutans and the humans will have to hang on as best they can. One thing that can be done right now, however, is to study the needs of these humanlike creatures and learn as much about them as possible in order to be better equipped to help them.

4

Research and Captivity

As RECENTLY AS the early 1960s, scientists knew little about the orangutan. During the last few decades of the twentieth century, knowledge about this elusive ape has increased dramatically. Everything that the world knows about *Pongo pygmaeus* is due to the efforts of scientists and researchers who have spent years living deep in the rain forests of Borneo and Sumatra. They engage in behavioral studies, recording and analyzing data about the orangutan's diet, habitat, reproduction, child-rearing methods, and interaction with its environment.

Just a few centuries ago, accurate population counts were nearly impossible to obtain for the orangutan because of its elusive nature and the remoteness of its habitat. Scientists can only make educated guesses based on fossils and random journal entries of early explorers who claimed to have seen them in certain remote locations. Methods of studying the animals in an accurate and scientific manner have only been developed and refined in the last few years. In fact, as recently as 1987 one researcher reported that the world population of orangutans was 179,000 apes. Three years later, at the sixty-fifth meeting of the IUCN's Species Survival Commission, a more scientifically credible source quoted the number at being between 30,000 and 50,000. Today, seemingly accurate census reports place it at a maximum of 27,000.

Before the 1960s, very little was known about the orangutan.

How it all began

The earliest recorded sighting of an orangutan by a Westerner dates back to 1658. During a trip to the islands of Southeast Asia, a man named Jacob Bontius described an orangutan in his journal. Two hundred years later, English naturalist Alfred Russel Wallace would be the first person to record critical observations of the animal. Wallace conducted some detailed studies of what the orangutan ate and how it lived. It was the first time any reliable information about the red ape was disseminated to the rest of the scientific community. Not until a century later would science again turn its critical eye to Borneo. In the 1960s John Mackinnon became the first modern researcher to devote time to the study of *Pongo pygmaeus*. A British zoologist, Mackinnon spent time in Sabah and northern Borneo, collecting volumes of information. In 1974 he published *In Search of the Red Ape,* which marked the general public's first major exposure to a detailed account of the orangutan's life. However, another researcher would do even more to focus attention on the orangutan.

Center stage

The arrival of Birute Galdikas on the research front heralded a new era of interest in the orangutan. Arriving in Kalimantan, Indonesia, in 1971, Galdikas set up camp and began research in the Tanjung Puting Forest. Early on, Galdikas vastly increased the body of knowledge about orangutans. She described their diets, foraging patterns, mating habits, and reproductive cycles. She was the first person to conduct a true long-term study of red apes. Living in the forests of Borneo for several years, she was able to collect data on a variety of topics that others had only touched on in the past. Galdikas documented the birth and weaning process of wild orangutans in great detail. She was also the first person to record male orangutans' long calls. Her research provided valuable information about orangutans' ecological needs and interconnections with their forest habitat.

Galdikas's greatest claim to fame, however, is probably what she did for the orangutan's public image. The Western world had been fascinated with accounts of chimpanzees and gorillas for quite some time, but in 1975 Galdikas appeared on the cover of *National Geographic* and wrote an article about her experiences with the orangutans of Indonesia. In 1980 *National Geographic* published a second story about her work. This time, the magazine's cover featured Galdikas's son, Binti, in a washbasin with one of his orangutan playmates. People seemed to love the stories and were hungry for more information about the mysterious apes. Galdikas knew that raising public interest, and money, would be the key to saving the endangered ape. She went on the lecture circuit, speaking at universities and providing interviews for a number of newspapers and magazines. She even

Nineteenth-century English naturalist Alfred Russel Wallace was the first person to record reliable information about the orangutan.

Pusaka

Birute Galdikas was one of the first people to conduct long-term studies of the orangutan. One of the difficulties that other researchers have faced was learning to communicate with and become accepted by the local people. Galdikas did not seem to have this problem. She became so entrenched in the culture that in 1981 she married a local Indonesian tribesman named Pak Bohap. One of the concepts that Galdikas had to grasp upon entering the local culture was *pusaka,* which, when roughly translated, means "power." The Dayaks, or native Borneans, will not deal with someone who has not demonstrated a certain amount of authority. Galdikas relies on the local people for help in running her rehabilitation facility, and she has to take part in a number of their ritualistic ceremonies in order to gain *pusaka* in their eyes. While her controlled, authoritative manner has helped in her dealings with the Dayaks, it has earned her a reputation as a self-styled dictator among many Western colleagues. Likewise, it has also made her a number of enemies, including poachers and Indonesian officials. Friends have expressed fear for Galdikas's safety; they claim that if she is not careful, she will find herself following in the footsteps of famed gorilla researcher Dian Fossey, who was murdered by local poachers.

appeared with Johnny Carson on the *Tonight Show* to promote her work. Never before had the orangutan been so much in the public eye.

Galdikas's efforts at raising awareness and rallying support for the red ape were well received. In 1982, partially due to her lobbying, the government of Indonesia declared the Tanjung Puting Forest a national park, affording it, and its inhabitants, complete protection. In 1984, Galdikas struck a deal with Earthwatch, a Boston-based educational travel program. The program sent tourists to help with Galdikas's research, and it added seventy thousand dollars a year to her efforts. In 1986 Galdikas founded the Orangutan Foundation International. Its stated purpose is to promote awareness and raise funds for the endangered orangutan. The widespread promotion of her research had permanently lifted the veil of obscurity that had long surrounded the orangutan.

Research challenges

While conducting behavioral research on orangutans may sound fun and exciting to most people, it does have its difficulties. The first major obstacle is usually securing finances. Research has to catch the attention of some well-endowed university or a private or governmental institution. By applying for monetary grants from these organizations, scientists are able to feed themselves as well as pay for facilities and buy the supplies that they need to conduct their work. Often grants are renewed with additional money, and that is generally a key to the success of a project. If a grant is not renewed, the research may come to a grinding halt.

Once finances are secured, the next challenge is to obtain a research permit from the Indonesian or Malaysian government. This can be difficult because these nations are often leery of the motives of Western researchers in their country. In addition, the Environmental Investigation Agency has reported that government officials will sometimes refuse to grant a permit without receiving some direct personal benefit. As a result, bribes and being connected to the right people are not uncommon parts of the permit acquisition process. To make matters worse, these governments have been known to revoke permits after researchers are already there and set up to work.

Once granted a permit, the researcher then faces the challenge of dealing with the unfamiliar customs of the local people. Whether buying goods or hiring guides, the researchers rely on the indigenous people in these areas for support, which means that scientists must be sensitive to long-held beliefs and traditions. Moreover, it is occasionally difficult to please both the government's bureaucrats and the local villagers. Primatologist Tom Struthsaker, who has spent time researching in Borneo, claims that "the

Louis Leakey

Human civilization has seen its share of men and women who have broken new ground in their fields and have swung wide the doors of progress and enlightenment. Louis Leakey was one such man. Leakey was an anthropologist obsessed with discovering the secrets of humankind's origins. He devoted his life to his research and made several groundbreaking fossil discoveries, including fragmentary remains of humanlike creatures that predated *Homo sapiens.* He showed the world how these early human ancestors probably looked, how they walked, and what kinds of tools they used. However, he was never satisfied with the amount of information that fossils could provide.

Leakey, who was fond of saying that behavior does not fossilize, wanted to know more about how early humans lived and interacted with each other. To learn more about the earliest ancestors of *Homo sapiens,* he proposed that researchers conduct long-term, multigenerational studies of humankind's closest living relatives: the apes. He believed that apes were probably closely related to early human ancestors, and by studying them, long-hidden secrets about humankind's past could be discovered. Most of Leakey's colleagues dismissed this idea, but he forged on. Under Leakey's guidance, several anthropologists made discoveries about ape behavior that led to a reexamination of what it means to be human. Among Leakey's proteges are Jane Goodall, who studied chimpanzees; Dian Fossey, who studied gorillas; and Birute Galdikas, who has devoted her life to studying orangutans. Louis Leakey died just a short time after sending Galdikas off to Borneo, but his legacy will undoubtedly live on.

Anthropologist Louis Leakey (left) felt that much could be learned about human behavior by studying apes.

social etiquette required to maneuver around people without offending officials is so subtle and intricate as to be impossible to understand, let alone master."[18] Galdikas recalls having to learn the local customs, and she claims that her ability to interact with them has allowed her to stay there as long as she has.

Jungle hazards

Once finances have been procured, permits cleared, and local help obtained, many researchers find that living in the dense rain forest can be a challenge all on its own. Most people can imagine the hazards of working in close quarters with large predators or poisonous snakes. The real danger, though, according to many field researchers, is actually from the tiniest predators that plague them on a daily basis: viruses, parasites, insects, and plant toxins. Galdikas, for example, reported having to remove countless leeches from her body every day. She also had to contend with mosquitoes, biting flies, fire ants, wolf spiders, black widows, and, perhaps worst of all, "tiny red ticks, looking like chili powder sprinkled on the skin, [that] bore their heads into the armpit, the back of the knees, and the groin, causing spasms akin to electrical shock every time the ticks were touched."[19]

The waiting game

Another challenge of orangutan research can be the frustration of having to spend much valuable time waiting to locate and then observe the apes. Orangutans can be extremely difficult to spot from the ground. Although their fur seems bright orange in a well-lit zoo enclosure, it appears as a dark shadow in the rain forest canopy. The apes blend in so well that novice researchers can hardly find them unless the orangutans happen to move. Once spotted, the waiting game continues. Orangutans are fairly inactive for a large part of each day. Waiting for some movement or activity can be a long, frustrating endeavor. According to Galdikas, "Compared with humans, chimpanzees, and most other primates, orangutans seem to operate in slow

motion. Years later, [renowned chimpanzee researcher] Jane Goodall commented that it took me two years to observe as much orangutan activity as she observed with chimpanzees in two hours."[20] The difficulties of orangutan behavioral research are many, but for patient researchers, so are the rewards. Behavioral studies, however, are not the only types of orangutan research currently being conducted.

An expert on ape behavior, Jane Goodall describes the plight of the orangutan at a press conference.

Census takers

One of the most important and difficult types of research involves counting how many orangutans really live in a given area. An accurate count is crucial in deciding where future logging and development will take place. No two researchers ever seem to come up with the same counts, but modern methods have brought estimates closer together.

Typically, an area is mapped out and divided into different habitat types or categories, such as lowland swamp, mountainous, or lowland forest. One sample area is selected from each category and a census is taken only in the

A Swamp of Their Own

Peat swamp forests cover about 20 percent of Borneo and are home to a number of primates and other animals, but they were not typically thought to house orangutans. A few years ago, however, Simon Husson of the University of Nottingham was leading a research team to assess the ecological importance of peat swamp forests when he came across a number of the apes. He set out to census the orangutans in the area and was able to determine that there were about two orangutans per square kilometer in his sample site. This figure is just slightly below the number found in the orangutan's favored habitats—lowland rain forests and freshwater swamp forests. These other forest types are not only favored by orangutans but also by loggers and farmers because of their valuable soil. Consequently, these more traditional ape habitats are the ones that are being destroyed. As a result of Husson's work, researchers are now aware that peat swamp forests can sustain orangutans. These areas, which are less desirable to humans, may be safe havens to transplant displaced orangutans. Satellite images have helped to determine that these peat swamps can viably sustain up to three thousand orangutans, which is at least 10 percent of the world's population.

selected areas. Since orangutans can be hard to spot, most researchers count the nests that they build for sleeping. Armed with a pair of binoculars, field assistants will attempt to locate as many nests as they can both from the ground and from above in helicopters. Researchers know about how often the apes will reuse the same nest before building a new one, so the number of nests can be translated into a number of orangutans for that specific sample area. This figure is then multiplied by the number of similar habitat types in the region. All the categories are then added together to provide an estimate of the local species population.

Unfortunately, this method often results in an overestimation of the population. The sample counts are usually conducted in areas known to have a number of orangutans, but the other areas of that type could be empty (due to poaching, disease, or a number of other causes). An additional problem is that the maps used to locate the different habitat types are almost always old and outdated; they do not reflect areas that have been recently deforested, for example. A recent conference on orangutan surveys has suggested that researchers use a new formula that will account for these factors. The conference found that simply multiplying the raw results by a factor of .75 seems to compensate for the stretches of empty forest.

GIS studies

Satellite imaging is also becoming a commonly used research tool. With the help of Geographical Information Systems (GIS), a computer program that encodes, analyzes, and displays spatial data, researchers are able to map the distribution of a species as well as plot and assess the impact of human encroachment on a given habitat.

The programmers enter detailed information on forest cover, roads, rivers, human settlements, soil conditions, harvesting and replanting patterns, and the distribution of plant and animal populations in a specific area. A computer then is used to create a map from these data. By entering proposed development plans into the program, technicians can create a computer simulation of the plan's ecological impact. In this way, development plans can be more accurately evaluated with regard to their effect on local wildlife before the project ever starts.

GIS mapping played a significant role in saving key orangutan habitat from development. Intensive GIS mapping of Sumatra's Gunung Leuser National Park was conducted in an effort to help direct proposed development in the region. Because this national park is extremely large, some groups claimed that dissecting it would cause little harm to the local wildlife. The GIS programmers performed simulations of several possible development plans, from simple road constructions to the complete erasure of all forested regions within the park. In all cases, the mapping showed that orangutan habitats would be significantly reduced, if not crippled. With a population of over nine thousand orangutans, the Greater Leuser area (which incorporates the park and its environs) is thought to be the primary stronghold of the world's Sumatran orangutan population. This area is critical to the survival of *Pongo pygmaeus abelii.* With the aid of this modern tool, the Gunung Leuser National Park may remain safe from development—at least for now.

In situ vs. ex situ

In addition to improving habitat management, field research also has useful applications in zoos. Research can be split into two distinct categories: in situ and ex situ. Literally translated, *in situ* means "in its original place" and refers to field studies. *Ex situ* translates as "out of its original place," and refers to studies conducted of animals in captivity. Many years of field research has added to scientists' understanding of orangutan behavior. All this information has helped conservationists, governments, and forestry workers to better provide for wild apes. In turn, these discoveries also help to improve conditions for orangutans in captivity. People have differing opinions about whether animals should be kept in captivity, but the fact remains that there are a large number of these apes in zoos, circuses, labs, and the entertainment industry around the world. It is the responsibility of their human caretakers to make use of the information gathered over the last few decades to help provide these captives with as healthy and fulfilling a life as possible. This sense of responsibility, however, is a relatively recent development.

The evolution of captivity

Orangutans have lived in captivity since the nineteenth century. Zoos and circuses of that era created exhibits designed for maximum shock value. People paid money to see freak shows, and at the time most people had never seen the wild animals of Africa and Asia. Consequently, many zoos and circuses created menageries, crowding as many of the mysterious beasts into their facility as possible. The proprietors knew little more than the public about the animals, and not surprisingly, the mortality rate of the more exotic animals, such as orangutans, was very high.

Today, most zoos have evolved into conservation institutions. The American Zoo and Aquarium Association (AZA), originally created in 1924, is an organization that grants accreditation to zoos that meet the AZA's Code of Professional Ethics. This code provides direction on ethical issues involving not only animal health and welfare but also a zoo's moral responsibility to its professional associates, employees, and the general public. Membership in the AZA is generally considered the official "seal of approval" for a zoological institution. Its members are urged to take an active role in conservation through breeding, education, and research.

Many zoos and circuses of the late nineteenth century were nothing more than a menagerie of assorted animals crowded into small areas.

Animal dating services

Zoos have been breeding orangutans for quite some time. The first recorded captive birth of an orangutan was in 1928 at the Philadelphia Zoo. Two Sumatrans, Maggie and Chief, gave birth to an infant. Unfortunately, the infant died shortly after its birth. Maggie never nursed it, and the zookeepers had no idea how to care for the infant themselves. Additional research, however, has improved the success rate; as of 1998, there have been 1,428 recorded births of orangutans in captivity, many of which have survived into adulthood.

Captive breeding has come a long way in the last seventy years. In 1981 the AZA created the Species Survival Plan (SSP). The SSP began as a cooperative population management and conservation program geared specifically for the captive propagation of endangered species. Each animal held in zoo collections and classified by the AZA as threatened or endangered has a long-term action plan created for it, which is managed by an SSP species coordinator. Likewise, a studbook keeper is responsible for maintaining detailed records on the breeding and life history of every captive orangutan in AZA institutions. The orangutan SSP species coordinator, along with the studbook keeper and an advisory committee, compiles a list of all orangutans held in zoos, including information on their sex, origin, subspecies, and breeding histories. A breeding program is then prepared that pairs unrelated individuals in order to maximize genetic diversity and prevent inbreeding. To facilitate this process, AZA zoos are often asked to lend animals to other zoos. According to SSP species coordinator Lori Perkins, the program's long-term goal is "to maintain in captivity a healthy, genetically-diverse, self-sustaining population of orangutans."[21] Thus, even if the wild population were to be completely wiped out due to habitat degradation, poaching, environmental disaster, or disease, a viable representation of the species would exist that could—in theory, at least—return to the wild someday.

Detractors of captive-breeding programs claim that they are simply not cost effective. One zoo, for example, quoted the yearly cost of caring for five species of primates at five hundred thousand dollars. This is the same amount of money it takes to operate an entire national park in some developing nations. Proponents of captive breeding, however, feel strongly that this concept may be the only chance to save some animals from extinction. Ulysses Seal, the chairman of the IUCN's Conservation Breeding Specialist Group, claims that at least captive breeding "provides options. If we don't do something now, then in thirty five

Reintroduction Plans

The Species Survival Plan is attempting to ensure that a self-sustaining population of captive orangutans will be around for many years to come and may someday be able to return to its native rain forest habitat. The release of captive and captive-born animals to the wild has been a hotbed of debate, and such programs have met with varying success. According to Ben Beck, a biologist at the National Zoo in Washington, D.C., 126 different species have been reintroduced into the wild. Of these, only 16 have been categorized as successful. Some opponents see this low success rate as evidence that reintroduction is not a viable option; others see reintroduction as a developing science in need of refinement. Orangutans that were born in the wild but raised in captivity have certainly been successfully returned to their native habitats. There are other success stories that provide inspiration to move along in this field: Reintroduction programs for the golden lion tamarin, the Arabian oryx, and the American bison, for example, have all met with a great deal of success. While the process of reintroduction may become more successful with time, there is still the question of cost. Ullas Karanth of the Center for Wildlife Studies in India points out that $30,000 a year would be enough money to pay for 50 guards to protect enough habitat for 250 to 300 lion-tailed macaques (another threatened primate). Reintroduction of just 12 of these same monkeys would cost $150,000. Apparently the debate will continue for quite some time, but without joint efforts to protect the orangutan's habitat and maintain its long-term survival and genetic diversity, there will be no hope at all.

years we will lose somewhere between one thousand and two thousand vertebrate species; they won't be around for the options to be tested."[22]

Education

Another major function of zoological parks is to promote awareness and educate the public about conservation issues affecting orangutans and other animals. By providing both information and the opportunity for a live encounter, zoos hope to reach people on a deeper level than other education mediums. The impact of such an experience typically goes much further than reading a book or watching a television program.

Today's zoos provide valuable information about the orangutan and many other animals to people of all ages.

It is becoming increasingly common to have volunteers or animal keepers posted outside orangutan exhibits to talk to the public about the animals. These animal caretakers often engage zoo guests in conversations about the orangutan's complex social and feeding behaviors, cognitive adaptations, and even habitat utilization. Through these informal discussions, zookeepers hope to bring the millions of people who visit their facilities each year closer to an understanding of, and subsequent connection with, the mysterious red ape. This connection is intended to stimulate people's interest in taking an active role in the orangutan's conservation. They are encouraged to do this in a variety of ways: Donating time or money to a conservation group or lobbying government officials for the reform of conservation laws. In some cases, these encounters may even spark the interest of young people, inspiring them to become research scientists or animal care professionals.

Research

Zoos also contribute to orangutan conservation through ex situ research. Keeping apes in a controlled environment, like that offered at modern zoos, allows researchers the freedom to closely observe their gestation periods, birthing, rearing, and physiology. Just as in situ studies help to provide information beneficial to captive animals, ex situ studies provide conservationists with information that helps them to better manage orangutan habitat in the wild. According to Melanie Bond, the North American studbook keeper for the orangutan SSP, "Growth and weight data, as well as dentition records from captive orangutans have been provided to help field workers determine [the] age of wild and ex-captive specimens."[23]

Another example of ex situ research comes from the work of William Karesh, who had formerly been a veterinarian at Seattle's Woodland Park Zoo. Using techniques and experience he gained at the zoo, Karesh has designed a special kind of dart that can be used to remove tissue samples from wild orangutans without immobilizing them. These samples are used for a variety of genetic tests. In the past, this procedure could only be done by shooting the animal with a tranquilizer. Tranquilizing a wild orangutan is always a dangerous procedure, though, because animals can be severely injured or even killed by an incorrect dosage of the anesthetizing agent or during their fall from the tree. Karesh's dart provides in situ researchers with a much safer option.

Cheryl Knott, a professor of anthropology at Harvard University, conducts research on wild orangutans in Kalimantan, Indonesia, and regularly uses captive studies to aid her research. Knott reports that she "uses urine samples of captive females to help [her] understand differences in hormonal levels between very well fed captive orangutans and wild orangutans."[24] She also uses the weight data collected for captive orangutan infants to help her determine exactly how physiologically

Weight data obtained from captive orangutans has been used to determine how physiologically burdensome it is for wild orangutan mothers to carry their young.

burdensome carrying infants is on wild orangutan mothers. This provides her with more data when studying the differences in habitat usage between orangutans with infants and those without.

Combining research and education

The National Zoo in Washington, D.C., has created an innovative program that combines research and education. The "Think Tank" is a research facility that studies cognition, or thinking, in orangutans and other animals. In 1995 this $4-million facility opened its doors to the public. Studies at the Think Tank have demonstrated the orangutan's prowess in solving problems and using tools. These studies have shown that the red ape can fashion rope from straw, select the appropriate key to unlock doors, and even dismantle parts of its cage to use as levers when prying something open. Researchers regularly stage problem-solving scenarios and observe the outcome; this helps them answer scientific questions, but it also encourages zoo guests to draw their own conclusions about whether the orangutans are truly thinking.

Just twenty-five years ago, the concept that some animals can think was shunned by scientists. It was a commonly held belief that humans were the only creatures who could think and use tools. This was justification for the notion that humans stood above the rest of the beasts. By introducing the average zoo guest to firsthand evidence of animals' thinking, the barriers between man and animal are slowly eroded and perhaps even awaken a new sense of responsibility in people to care for their not-so-distant relatives.

5

The Future

THE FUTURE OF the orangutan remains uncertain. The species faces many challenges in the coming years. Ironically, its only real predator has also become its greatest hope for survival. Humans have hunted the orangutan, plucked it from the forest, and destroyed its habitat, causing the ape to become critically endangered. However, humans are now beginning to attempt repairs on the damage they have done. Governments, private organizations, and individuals have begun a number of initiatives to save the orangutan, but they are spending a lot of money and resources on a war that some say is already lost. The question now remains: Should valuable time, energy, and money be spent to save the orangutan?

Some people argue that extinction is a natural process and should be allowed to run its course. According to the nineteenth-century biologist Charles Darwin, the process of evolution requires that species less "fit" to survive give way to those that are better adapted. If the human race is more fit to survive and is able to dominate the habitat, then perhaps the orangutan is simply losing the battle of natural selection. Species, the argument holds, have come and gone for hundreds of millions of years.

There are certainly arguments against this point. For example, within the natural order of things, extinction is typically a gradual process that occurs over a period of thousands of years. The orangutan, however, has gone from being a stable, viable species to being nearly extinct in just one century. Conservation proponents would also

Charles Darwin's "survival of the fittest" theory has been used to argue that it is natural to allow the orangutan to become extinct.

argue that just because humans *can* dominate something does not mean they *should*. The human brain, they contend, possesses the ability to project long-term consequences. This ability has aided the survival of the human race, but conservationists would argue that with this ability comes the burden of taking responsibility for actions that affect other species.

The importance of an orangutan

Morality aside, there are other, more practical reasons for saving the orangutan from extinction. The red ape's very presence, in some ways, is a key to protecting all the rain forests of Southeast Asia. People are becoming more aware that all life on earth, including humans, are completely dependent on these forests for survival. The world's rain forests have provided humankind with a number of products they often take for granted: coffee, chocolate, rubber, and about half of all medicines in the world today. Of course, many of these items can now be artificially produced outside of the forest. However, the vast majority of the world's rain forest plants have yet to be studied. There is no way to tell how many more medicines, natural pesticides, and foods are waiting to be found. Once the forests are gone, these undiscovered treasures will be lost forever.

The orangutan plays an important role in protecting these vital rain forest resources. Most rain forests are closed systems, which means the entire ecosystem operates as one large organism. The plants, fungi, and animals are all completely interconnected and dependent on each other for survival. The combined interactions of these smaller organisms make up the rain forest. The orangutan is an integral part of this system. By eating a large amount

The Lungs of the Earth

Since the orangutan acts as a keystone species, protecting it usually equates to protecting the entire rain forest. Saving the rain forest is absolutely vital to the survival of all life on the earth. The rain forest serves as the lungs of the earth. The huge green belt of forest that runs along the equator is largely responsible for converting the carbon dioxide in the world's atmosphere into oxygen. If fewer trees exist, more carbon dioxide will remain in the atmosphere. The reduction of the world's rain forest has already noticeably affected the planet's environment.

A recent increase in carbon dioxide levels has caused what scientists refer to as the greenhouse effect. A canopy of carbon dioxide is beginning to build up over the planet. This layer lets the heat from the sun's rays pass through the atmosphere but does not allow all of the heat back out, trapping it at the earth's surface. If this trend continues, scientists believe that the polar ice caps will eventually melt, raising the sea level all over the world and submerging large portions of the earth's landmass. Thus, the benefits of saving the orangutan and its habitat are quite far-reaching.

Protecting the earth's rain forests and the plant and animal life found there is essential to preserving the earth's environment.

of ripe fruits, the orangutan serves as a seed disburser. In fact, some trees depend solely on the orangutan to distribute their seeds throughout the forest. Furthermore, by eating buds, shoots, and leaves, the orangutan effectively thins out, or prunes, the forest, allowing sunlight to come through the canopy and stimulate growth in the understory.

Orangutans are also messy eaters, which means that they serve as a food delivery service for many of the ground-dwelling creatures. As the orangutan drops uneaten portions of fruit to the ground below, a variety of smaller animals and insects are treated to a free meal. These scraps make up the bulk of many rain forest animals' diets.

Perhaps the most important role the orangutan plays in the forest, however, is as a "keystone" species. A keystone species is one that has, for one reason or another, caught the attention of the human world and acts as a focal point for forest protection. Orangutans are large, attractive, interesting, and perceived as highly intelligent. They are also seen as a close relative to the human species. For all these reasons, people are interested in saving them. Thus, in the course of saving orangutans, people also unwittingly save the lives of countless species of smaller animals, insects, and plants that share their habitat. By rallying behind efforts to protect orangutans, the general public helps to preserve complete ecosystems.

Marketing the orangutan

Just as large corporations advertise their commercial products, conservationists are now beginning to use the tools of mass media to spark interest in their causes. Since the mid-1980s, the world has focused an enormous amount of attention on conservation and wildlife. People have been exposed to the orangutan and its plight through an ever-increasing swell of media attention. Magazine articles, television programs, books, and entire cable networks devoted to wildlife have made this information available to many people. Several major motion pictures have featured orangutans; while some animal rights groups claim that this is exploitive, the fact remains that these movies create widespread interest in the animal.

The animal's public image is further enhanced by the involvement of television and movie personalities in conservation efforts. Movie star Julia Roberts, for example, recently hosted a prime-time TV special with Birute Galdikas on orangutan rehabilitation efforts in the wilds of Borneo. According to an article in the May 1998 issue of *Life* magazine, "When filmmakers Andrew Jackson and Nigel Cole recruited Julia Roberts to star in their documentary . . . they hoped her Hollywood luster would help spotlight the animal's predicament."[25] The show received an enormous public response. The success of marketing efforts such as these has led to an increased public interest in the red ape. This interest has provided the incentive and, in many cases, the funding to establish a wide range of new orangutan conservation initiatives.

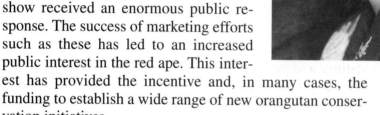

Actress Julia Roberts has played an active role in efforts to save the orangutan.

Wanariset

A number of new organizations have been created during the last few years to aid in the preservation of orangutans. The Balikpapan Orangutan Society (BOS) is a nonprofit group whose mission is to give financial support to the Wanariset Orangutan Reintroduction Center (WORC). The BOS was founded by Willie Smits, the senior adviser to Indonesia's minister of forestry. Since its inception, the group has been actively involved in local outreach education and in attempts to increase worldwide recognition of the current orangutan crisis. The BOS has raised large sums of money to support the WORC's efforts.

Originally, the Wanariset Forestry Research Station was established to "contribute to the conservation and wise utilization of tropical rain forests with research of a practical nature."[26] The station continues to study the tropical ecology of the plant and animal species of Indonesian rain forests, including the biology, behavior, and needs of the orangutan.

At Wanariset, a baby orangutan recovers from the effects of inhaling smoke from the Borneo wildfires.

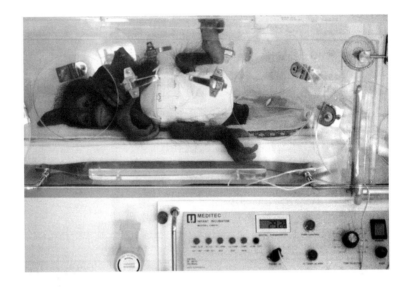

Its in-depth studies focus on topics such as parasites, disease resistance, heartbeat ratios and body temperatures under varying conditions, and weight development in relation to food intake.

As the research progressed, the Indonesian government began giving the research station formerly captive orangutans to rehabilitate and release into the forest. This duty became more time consuming, and the WORC was created as an offshoot of the forestry research station. Established in 1991, the center follows the rehabilitation methods of Herman Rijksen and is considered a state-of-the-art facility. Twenty-five percent of the center's funding comes from the Indonesian government; the rest comes from the fund-raising efforts of the BOS.

Release sites

The WORC is considered to be one of the most successful reintroduction centers in Indonesia, and it is currently involved in releasing a large number of orangutans into appropriate habitats. It is now law in Indonesia that formerly captive orangutans must be released in areas without existing wild populations. This prevents complications from overcrowding and the transmission of disease from the former captives to the resident populations. The challenge is to find an area that has no native orangutans, has the appropriate type of habitat, is large enough to support long-term release efforts, and has not been slated for logging or agricultural conversion.

The WORC has found two excellent release sites. The first, called Sungai Wain, is a twenty-seven-thousand-acre protected forest. It is completely isolated from humans by crocodile-infested swampland, and the only human access to the forest is via a cable car system suspended overhead, which reduces the likelihood of poaching. This forest is also crucial to the water supply of the city of Balikpapan. According to the BOS, "The water flow for the city can be sustained only when this forest remains inviolate."[27] Consequently, there is little chance of it being cleared for agriculture. The Sungai Wain release site has been very successful so far, with a survival rate of approximately 80 percent.

The other primary release site is known as the Meratus Forest. Surrounding the Meratus Mountains, these rain forest–covered foothills abound with fruit trees and are home to a number of creatures that often share habitat with orangutans. The presence of bears, civets, birds, and gibbons suggests that this area is the perfect habitat for orangutans. The release area within Meratus is approximately 50,000 acres, and it is surrounded by another 2.5 million acres of forest. The outlook in other parts of Borneo, however, is less encouraging.

Isolated from humans by crocodile-infested swamps, Sungai Wan is an ideal release site for rehabilitated orangutans.

Other Bornean regions

Kalimantan, the largest region on Borneo, is home to most of the world's orangutans, but it is also the area where they are most threatened. Kalimantan has a large human population that is growing every day. The human settlements are often located close to the forest. As a result, the bulk of the orangutan pet trade is supplied from this region. This is also the area most heavily hit by the wildfires of 1997–1998. Fully one-half (or 718,000 acres) of the Kutai National Park has already been burned to the ground. Nearly 8,000 acres of Sungai Wain have also been razed by the fires. In fact, during just the first five months of 1998, more than 1.2 million acres of Borneo's rain forest habitat were consumed by flame. The World Wildlife Fund estimates that one thousand orangutan babies, fleeing from the fires, have been captured by local poachers in Kalimantan. This figure, of course, represents another thousand mothers that were shot to obtain the youngsters.

Even the well-known Tanjung Puting National Park, the home of Camp Leakey, is not immune to problems. Ecotourist guidebooks claim that the area remains mostly wild and untouched. However, the IUCN has recently listed it as an endangered region. Its borders are surrounded by gold mines and oil and gas wells. These operations are upsetting the park's ecosystem and attracting an ever-increasing swell of migrant workers. Despite its status as one of the better-protected parks in Indonesia, one Tanjung Puting ranger reported having seen seven orangutan infants confiscated from poachers during a period of just a few weeks.

Sumatran survey

While the orangutan's future in Borneo may be uncertain, its future in Sumatra is even more tenuous. According to Ron Tilson, a researcher from the Minnesota Zoo, "There are sixteen major protected areas inhabited by orangutans. Fifteen of these areas . . . are on the island of Borneo."[28] The only officially protected habitat for the Sumatran orangutan is the Gunung Leuser National Park. Although several other Sumatran reserves are home to

Birute's Battles

Birute Galdikas is known for having conducted the first long-term behavioral study of orangutans. She made groundbreaking discoveries about how they fed, traveled, socialized, gave birth, and reared their young. For a number of years Galdikas was the orangutan's most outspoken advocate and probably did more than any other person to bring their plight to the world's attention. In recent years, however, she has been accused of allowing her attachment to her subjects cloud her judgment.

In the early 1980s Galdikas began to shift her focus away from orangutan research to concentrate on rehabilitation efforts. She has defied Indonesian officials on many occasions, and she continues to use rehabilitation methods that are considered "questionable" by government authorities and even other scientists. On several occasions the government has suspended her permit to work in Camp Leakey. During these times, Galdikas would gather up her charges and take them to her private home. There, she has been accused of subjecting the apes to overcrowding and filthy, unsanitary conditions. She has also been accused of becoming irrational and of treating her helpers as servants.

In 1994 the Earthwatch organization, which had provided Galdikas with over seventy thousand dollars a year in funding, pulled its support and ceased to sponsor ecotourist trips to her facility. Many members of the scientific community have begun to disregard Galdikas's work. Peter S. Rodman, a well-known anthropologist from the University of California at Davis, refers to her as "something of a scientific non-entity."

Despite her lack of research, allegations of unsafe rehabilitation methods, and her knack for alienating many of her colleagues, Galdikas forges on in defense of the red ape. She continues to receive some support as well. In 1997 the president of Indonesia awarded Galdikas the "Hero of the Earth" award, and an article in the May 1998 issue of *Life* magazine described her as the orangutan's most determined ally. When questioned about the lack of hard science underlying her research, Galdikas once responded, "When a species is threatened with extinction, I don't understand how anyone can say it is more important to study than to save it."

known populations of orangutans, they do not have officially protected status. The Singkil Barat Reserve consists of extensive swamp forests that are ideal for the red apes. However, there are conflicting reports as to how badly disturbed the habitat has become. There are a small number of

A young orangutan wades in the swamp forest of the Singkil Barat Reserve.

orangutans in the Sebabala–Dolok Sembelin population, but it is currently in an area designated as production forest and is slated for development through logging and agricultural conversion. There are also unconfirmed reports of a small population of orangutans in western Sumatra, but this has yet to be investigated.

By far, the largest population of Sumatran orangutans exists in the Greater Leuser area. A subsection of this region is the Gunung Leuser National Park. Currently, the park's orangutans are divided into two distinct subpopulations. The eastern population has about thirty-five hundred orangutans, and the western group is thought to number fifty-seven hundred. This split is strictly maintained by the presence of a major road that runs through the center of the park. Human activity, including settlements, have sprung up all along the road, creating an effective barrier between the two orangutan groups. Carel Van Schaik of Duke University and his colleagues believe that this split is not a serious problem because each subpopulation is large enough to remain viable. However, these scientists are quick to point out that any further fragmentation of the park could seriously threaten the future of Sumatra's last stronghold of wild orangutans.

Conferences

As research projects and worldwide interest in orangutans continue to grow, more collaborative efforts to address the animals' problems have begun. In 1993 the IUCN's Species Survival Commission sponsored the

Orangutan Population and Habitat Viability Analysis Report. This was an exhaustive study by the commission's Conservation Breeding Specialist Group. The results were presented in October of that year in Medan, Indonesia. The project's goals were to assess the current status of the wild orangutans and assemble all unpublished information to assist in the development of strategies for the management of the species. The group reported on and quantified the major threats to the wild population of orangutans. It also used computer simulations to estimate the future impact of certain types of land development projects. In addition, it identified the most important areas for the Indonesian government to concentrate its efforts. By protecting these areas—Gunung Leuser in Sumatra; Kutai, Tanjung Puting, Kendawangan, Gunung Palung, and Gunung Nyuit in Borneo—the governments would be helping to provide viable habitats for most of the remaining animals. Efforts continue on behalf of the orangutans, and not just in their home countries of Indonesia and Malaysia.

The neglected ape

In March 1994 the California State University at Fullerton hosted an international conference called "Orangutans: The Neglected Ape." Organized by the university's department of anthropology, the Zoological Society of San Diego, and the Atlanta/Fulton County Zoo (now known as Zoo Atlanta), the conference represented a collaboration between zoological parks and university researchers. A number of papers were presented on a wide variety of topics relating to orangutans, including conservation, behavior, captive breeding, cognition, genetics, and veterinary medicine.

Willie Smits presented a paper on his new methods of rehabilitation, and Isabelle Lardeux-Gilloux presented one on the history and future of rehabilitation centers. One Kyoto University researcher, Akira Suzuki, even presented detailed information on the aftermath of fires in Kalimantan during 1982 and 1983, explaining how the fires had affected feeding and behavior patterns. This paper turned out to have great significance to future conservation planning,

What Scientists Have Always Known

Sometimes the wheels of progress can be slow to move. Terry Maple, the director of Zoo Atlanta, claims that conservationists have long known what is needed to save the orangutan. According to Maple, a report published in 1937 lists recommendations for protecting the ape. Suggestions include a complete ban on killing or capturing orangutans. The report also suggests that when large tracts of land are given over to logging or development, the resident orangutans should be relocated rather than captured or killed. It even mentions the importance of educating local people and the military on issues surrounding the ape and its importance.

Some corners of the scientific community were apparently aware of the orangutan's impending doom. This information, however, was not widely available or publicized. The general public had little knowledge of, or concern for, the ape. It was not until nearly a half century later that people began to take notice. Perhaps the wheels of progress have been sped up enough to save the orangutan before it is too late.

as Kalimantan was again ravaged by fires just three years after the conference. The result of this conference was an increased body of knowledge across several different disciplines that would eventually aid each of the participating researchers and conservationists in efforts to protect the orangutan from extinction.

"The Politics of Extinction"

In July 1998 the Environmental Investigation Agency (EIA) published "The Politics of Extinction," a detailed investigative report about the current threats to the wild orangutan population and the destruction of Indonesia's forests. The report stated that despite increased efforts to protect habitat, such as improved forest management and a decline in timber exports, Indonesia still supplies the world with 40 percent of its plywood.

One of the industries most destructive to the orangutan's habitat, according to the EIA, is the production of palm oil. The global demand for this product has apparently been skyrocketing during the late 1990s. It now competes in the world market with more traditional oils, such as sunflower seed and soy. In 1996 palm oil accounted for 52 percent of the market. The price per ton went from $562 to $705 in just one year. Indonesia's climate is perfect for palm plantations, and with its economy in trouble, it cannot pass up the opportunity to become a major player in this market. Currently, Indonesia and Malaysia together produce over 80 percent of the world's palm oil. Indonesia is planning to increase its plantations from 2.4 million hectares to 5.5 million by the year 2000. These enormous increases in agricultural conversion may be the most devastating of all current threats to the orangutan's habitat.

Each new plantation represents a stretch of fertile forest that has been cut and burned. In addition, the EIA report claims that up to 80 percent of the forest fires that ravaged large tracts of the red ape's habitat were caused by commercial palm oil and pulpwood plantations. In fact, the fires have caused the price of palm oil to go up even further—about 10 percent—by destroying a large part of the palm oil supply. And this price increase just provides more incentive to create new plantations.

Forestry reforms

One of the biggest problems for orangutans has been the failure of the Indonesian government to regulate the country's forestry industry. According to the EIA, former long-term Indonesian president T. N. J. Suharto was repeatedly criticized for absolving wealthy friends in the logging industry of the penalties they incurred as a result of breaking timber-harvesting laws. In 1991, for example, Barito Pacific was fined $4 million for logging outside its concession area, but the company simply refused to pay the fine and continued its logging practices.

Suharto is no longer in power, and the government formed by his successor is trying to erase some of the damage done to the nation's forests by enacting stricter regulations. Indonesia's Ministry of Forestry now grants land concessions in plots of 250,000 acres. Each plot is divided

Former Indonesian president Suharto often absolved his wealthy friends of penalties resulting from their violations of logging restrictions.

into thirty-five blocks, only one of which may be harvested each year. Each concessionaire is required to pay sixteen dollars per cubic meter of harvested timber to fund a national reforestation campaign. They must also pay an additional dollar per cubic meter to finance an inventory mapping system. This inventory system involves aerial photography, satellite imaging, and ground surveys to help effectively monitor Indonesia's vast expanse of forest.

All timber harvesting must also follow the new reduced impact logging guidelines. These guidelines include three major focal points. The first is selective logging. Only five to six trees per hectare are to be removed . Second, and some researchers say most important, are methods to reduce the impact of secondary damage that occurs to smaller tress when large trees are felled.

The third major component of the guidelines is replanting young trees in the area where full-grown ones have been extracted. The area is then to be left untouched for thirty-five years so that the saplings are allowed to grow. In this way, the resources are considered sustainable since they will continually replenish themselves. In theory, these harvesting methods should cause little damage to the ecosystems, allowing the plants and animals to thrive even in areas slated for development.

Marginal success

Although the government of Indonesia has demonstrated some commitment to the preservation of its native forest habitats, it has been only marginally successful in enforcing the new regulations. For example, one of the regulations states that only trees with more than a fifty-centimeter diameter may be harvested. The World Bank, however, reports that only 2.2 percent of the logs ever go through the legally required measurement verifications. When the inspections are conducted, many timber companies fail to meet the established criteria. Indonesia's Ministry of Forestry reported that from 1992 to 1993, 84 percent of timber concession holders failed to meet the regulations. As recently as 1996, this same office stated that 70 percent of timber coming into Jakarta (Indonesia's capital) was illegal. Regulators point out that they do attempt to take action. A 1996 crackdown resulted in the detention of eighty-three timber ships. Recently, four hundred illegal loggers and a plywood mill were discovered operating in the Tanjung Puting National Park; they were eventually removed by the military.

Most of the government's attempts have been thwarted due to economics. There is one forestry staff member for every 127,000 hectares of forest. Corruption among officials also continues to be a challenge. In 1996, for instance, fifteen illegal log barges were impounded, but they soon "disappeared" in two separate incidents. Without some cooperation from the timber industry itself, government regulation will never succeed. Fortunately, just such a commitment has begun to surface.

Corruption among Indonesian government officials was responsible for the "disappearance" of fifteen illegal log barges seized in 1996.

ITTO

The International Tropical Timber Organization (ITTO) is currently working on a plan to develop an internationally recognized eco-labeling system for wood products. Organization members hope the plan will go into effect by the year 2000. Similar to labeling paper products as "made from recycled materials," this seal would let the public know that the purchase of a wood product is supporting an environmentally responsible company. The Indonesian government is working with the ITTO and hopes to have this seal affixed to their wood products. This stamp would act as a marketing tool by increasing sales and thus bringing in more money. This increased revenue would help the government justify all the "inconvenient and costly" harvesting regulations it is imposing on the timber industries working within the country.

Local involvement

In addition to regulating and enlisting the help of local industries, an important aspect of protecting orangutan habitats is changing the attitudes of the people who live and work in these areas. The local people often harbor resentment towards these initiatives. They see all of the laws that are being created to protect habitats and orangutans as interfering with their own lifestyles. Many people see it as an orangutan-versus-human issue, and they do not appreciate their government taking the side of the apes. According to zoologist John Mackinnon, if the indigenous people do not want to save the rain forest, it cannot be saved. They must be made to see a value in its protection. He suggests that the rehabilitation centers be renamed "conservation stations" and be used as focal points for garnering support from local people.

The locals are intensely curious about what goes on in these facilities. Many of the rehabilitation centers take advantage of this fact by inviting people in to learn about the work there. The workers at the centers provide the local people with basic education about wildlife management and why it is so important to protect the animals and their habitats. Annelisa Kilbourn makes a regular practice of this at the Sepilok Wildlife Center in Malaysia's state of Sabah. Since many local Malaysians have long been at war with their orangutan neighbors, Kilbourn believes that this interaction and education are critical to the survival of orangutans. The residents of Sabah must guard their crops from local orangutans, who have learned to come into town and raid the harvests. These people often fend off the apes with clubs and machetes, leaving many of them injured and in need of Kilbourn's care at the center. Since these education efforts have begun, the locals often call on the Sepilok staff to trap raiding orangutans instead of killing or attacking the apes themselves.

Ecotourism

Another way to convince the local people of the importance of orangutan protection is to show them a cash value in it. By opening rehabilitation centers to Western tourists, the locals benefit from the money the visitors spend during their visits. In some areas, locals are even included in the planning and design of these tourist programs. Local people are hired as guides, attendants, and cooks, thereby providing them with paying jobs. In some cases, local villages are even given a fixed percentage of the incoming funds to be disbursed as they see fit. Indonesia's director general of tourism claims that ecotourism can "provide a self-financing mechanism for the conservation of the natural heritage through proper management and ecological control."[29]

Although it is tempting to see ecotourism as a cure-all for the orangutan's problems, the practice is not without its own complications. Ecotourism has become extremely popular among Westerners, and there is no shortage of people who want to visit these facilities. They are lured to Indonesia and Malaysia with the promise of seeing baby orangutans being nursed to health, trained, and released back into their forest homes. How close their actual experi-

A young ecotourist poses with an orangutan and her baby.

ence comes to that has been a topic of some controversy. There is some concern over the potentially negative impact these tourists may have on the animals in rehabilitation. First, they can bring foreign disease into the camps. Since the apes are susceptible to human disease, there is a danger that they could easily carry a dangerous pathogen back into the wild, thereby sowing the seeds of an epidemic. Birute Galdikas, though, is quick to point out that she has been having foreigners visit her camp for many years with no incidence of epidemics.

In addition, some rehabilitation workers fear that the increased flow of human traffic may undermine their efforts to break the former captives' reliance on people. Most facilities that take part in these programs now have strict protocols prohibiting any physical contact between the tourists and the orangutans. However, this is another area where written policy does not always match reality. Many people have been interviewed about their experience upon leaving the country and report the highlight as being allowed to hold a baby orangutan. According to Herman Rijksen, these interactions with tourists serve to remind the orangutans that humans are a ready source of food and comfort. The result is that "all the months of training we gave the animals to become wild again [can be] broken in a day."[30] There are undeniable benefits of continuing these ecotourist programs: economic gain and an increased interest from local people in protecting the orangutan and its habitat. However, these gains must be weighed against the potential threat of undermining the very purpose of the rehabilitation centers.

The future

The governments of Indonesia and Malaysia are beginning to make the preservation of orangutans and their habitat a priority. They have demonstrated this new attitude through reform of their forestry industry, laws protecting habitat, and attempts to reduce the illegal trade in orangutans. They seem committed to enacting change. The government of Indonesia, for example, currently offers scholarships for Indonesian students who want to study forestry science and wildlife management. In this way, the governments are attempting to ensure that there will always be a pool of well-trained experts to wisely manage their vast forest resources. Indonesian schoolchildren have even gotten involved in supporting the local rehabilitation centers in their areas. They stage fundraisers and wage letter-writing campaigns to wealthy industrialists to ask for support.

All of these efforts, however, will be useless without the assistance of developed nations. Both Indonesia and Malaysia are in dire economic straits. Their governments resent the hypocrisy of other countries who chastise them for their inability to properly manage their forests; after all, most of the Indonesian and Malaysian logging products are purchased by developed nations that have depleted their own natural resources.

Despite efforts to save the orangutan, the red ape's future remains precarious.

Clearly, the orangutan's future is precarious. The fact that the ape's salvation is now in the hands of the same species that nearly caused its elimination seems somehow appropriate. Saving the orangutan from its unsteady perch at the edge of extinction will be a difficult battle. The amount of time, energy, and money that the world is willing to focus on *Pongo pygmaeus* seems to be the deciding factor in whether the orangutan survives into the future.

Notes

Chapter 1: The Red Ape

1. Quoted in Mark Starowicz, "Leakey's Last Angel," *New York Times Magazine,* August 16, 1992, p. 31.

Chapter 2: Pets and Rehabilitation

2. Quoted in Victoria J. Taylor and Nigel Dunstone, eds., *The Exploitation of Mammal Populations.* London: Chapman & Hall, 1996, p. 5.

3. Balikpapan Orangutan Society, "Orangutans at Risk." www.redcube.nl/bos/bos.htm.

4. Quoted in Steve Kuznik, "How to Be an Orangutan," *International Wildlife,* January/February 1997, p. 38.

5. Quoted in Kuznik, "How to Be an Orangutan," p. 38.

6. Quoted in Kuznik, "How to Be an Orangutan," p. 38.

7. Quoted in Jacqueline J. Ogden, Lorraine A. Perkins, and Lori Sheeran, *The Proceedings of the International Conference on Orangutans: The Neglected Ape.* San Diego: Zoological Society of San Diego, 1994, p. 42.

8. Quoted in Ogden, Perkins, and Sheeran, *The Proceedings of the International Conference on Orangutans,* p. 42.

9. Quoted in Taylor and Dunstone, *The Exploitation of Mammal Populations,* p. 9.

Chapter 3: Habitat Loss

10. World Wildlife Fund (press release), "Indonesian Fires' Distress Leads People to Kill Orangutans," October 30, 1997. www.panda.org/news/press/news_161.htm.

11. Quoted in Kuznik, "How to Be an Orangutan," p. 38.

12. Quoted in Thomas Fuller, "Forests Die as Borneo Prays for Rain," *International Herald Tribune,* April 20, 1998.

13. Fuller, "Forests Die as Borneo Prays for Rain."

14. Quoted in World Wildlife Fund (press release), "Indonesian Fires' Distress Leads People to Kill Orangutans."

15. Quoted in *Associated Press,* "US and World Report: Indonesia–Orangutans," November 11, 1997.

16. Quoted in Balikpapan Orangutan Society, News Update. www.redcube.nl/bos/news.htm.

17. Quoted in Fuller, "Forests Die as Borneo Prays for Rain."

Chapter 4: Research and Captivity

18. Quoted in Sy Montgomery, *Walking with the Great Apes.* Boston: Houghton Mifflin, 1991, p. 211.

19. Birute Galdikas, "Waiting for Orangutans," *Discover,* December 1994, p. 102.

20. Galdikas, "Waiting for Orangutans," p. 104.

21. Lori Perkins, interview with the author, March 31, 1999.

22. Quoted in *International Wildlife,* "Should We Put Them All Back?" September/October 1993, p. 39.

23. Melanie Bond, interview with the author, March 31, 1999.

24. Cheryl Knott, interview with the author, April 1, 1999.

Chapter 5: The Future

25. Kenneth Miller and Alan Sheldon, "Saving the Last Orangutans," *Life,* May 1998, p. 66.

26. Balikpapan Orangutan Society, "Research at Wanariset Station." www.redcube.nl/bos/research.htm.

27. Balikpapan Orangutan Society, "About the Rainforest." www.redcube.nl/bos/forest.htm.

28. Ronald Tilson, ed., *Orangutan Population and Habitat Viability Analysis Report.* Indonesia: IUCN Species Survival Commission, October 23, 1993.

29. Quoted in Rachel Drewry, "Ecotourism: Can It Save the Orangutan?" *Inside Indonesia.* www.serve.com/inside/.

30. Quoted in Kuznik, "How to Be an Orangutan," p. 38.

Glossary

arboreal: The term used to describe an animal that spends the bulk of its life in the trees.

AZA: The American Zoo and Aquarium Association; an organization that was created to share information and set standards for proper care and treatment of captive animals.

census: A count or tally of a specific population.

CITES: Convention on International Trade in Endangered Species; a regulatory group that decides, through the mutual agreement of its members, on international policies.

clear-cutting: The practice of felling all the trees in a section of forest at the same time.

Dayak: Collective name for a group of indigenous people who inhabit the island of Borneo.

ecosystem: A biologically balanced environment formed by the interaction of plants and animals.

ecotourism: The booming industry that provides nature-oriented vacations in national parks, reserves, and wildlife rescue centers.

endangered species: A type of plant or animal that is nearing extinction.

ex situ: A term meaning "out of its original place"; used to specify actions or research that takes place in captivity.

extinction: The complete and permanent elimination of a plant or animal species.

fitness: A term used to describe an animal's likelihood of reproducing.

flanges: The large flaps of skin that develop on the sides of an adult male orangutan's face.

forage: To search an environment for food.

genetic diversity: A healthy recombination of DNA that allows a species to thrive and develop throughout time.

habitat: The locality or living space of a plant or animal.

in situ: A term meaning "in its original place"; used to specify actions or research that takes place in the wild.

IUCN: International Union for the Conservation of Nature and Natural Resources, sometimes called the World Conservation Union; an organization that conducts research and makes recommendations on conservation issues throughout the world.

Kalimantan: An Indonesian province on the island of Borneo.

keystone species: An animal that has the ability to act as a focal point for conservation initiatives.

mias: Dayak term meaning "orangutan."

poaching: The illegal hunting or capture of an animal.

Pongo pygmaeus: The genus and species name for the orangutan.

propagation: Reproduction.

Sabah: A Malaysian state on the island of Borneo.

Sarawak: A Malaysian state on the island of Borneo.

SSC: The IUCN's Species Survival Commission; a group of scientists who conduct research on the long- and short-term conservation issues affecting threatened species.

SSP: Species Survival Plan; a plan drawn up by the AZA to help ensure the future of selected species through tightly controlled captive-breeding programs.

sustainable development: Utilizing an area's resources without destroying them.

Organizations
to Contact

Balikpapan Orangutan Society (BOS)
Orangutan Reintroduction Project
PO Box 447
Balikpapan 76103
Kalimantan Timur, Indonesia
(62 542) 413 069
website: www.redcube.nl/bos/default.htm

The BOS is a nonprofit organization whose mission is to provide financial support to the Wanariset Orangutan Reintroduction Center, to support outreach education locally, and to increase worldwide recognition of the current problems faced by the orangutan.

Environmental Investigation Agency (EIA)
PO Box 53343
Washington, DC 20009
(202) 483-6621
e-mail: eiaus@igc.apc.org

Established in 1984, the EIA is an organization dedicated to investigating and exposing wildlife abuse and campaigning to prevent it. Known for its aggressive techniques, the agency has exposed a number of illegal activities both in governments and private industry.

Orangutan Foundation International (OFI)
822 S. Wellesley Ave.
Los Angeles, CA 90049
(800) ORANGUTAN
website: www.ns.net/orangutan/index1.html

Founded by Birute Galdikas, the organization is dedicated to research, conservation, and education. The foundation helps to disseminate information about orangutans and their habitat, and it has several publications and an extremely informative website.

Primate Information Network (PIN)
Attn: Larry Jacobsen
Library Sciences
Primate Center Library
Wisconsin Regional Primate Research Center
Madison, WI 53715-1299
(608) 263-3515
website: www.primate.wisc.edu/pin/

This is an extensive website for anyone interested in the field of primate studies. The site is maintained by the Wisconsin Regional Primate Research Center and serves as an information gathering and distributing tool for students, scientists, and primate caretakers. There is information on current research in the field, a copy of the World Directory of Primatologists, information on careers in primatology, and a bulletin board system for scientific exchange.

SSC Primate Specialist Group
Attn: Dr. Russell A. Mittermeier
Conservation International
2501 M St. NW, Suite 200
Washington, DC 20037
(202) 429-5660
e-mail: r.mittermeier@conservation.org

The Species Survival Commission (SSC) is a branch of the IUCN that assesses the dynamics of biodiversity through the study of plant and animal species. It is composed of seven thousand scientists who contribute to this research in their particular field of expertise. It is divided into several specialist groups. The Primate Specialist Group produces several newsletters about its work, including *Primate Conservation, Asian Primates, African Primates,* and *Neotropical Primates.*

United Nations Environment Programme (UNEP)
DC2-0803
United Nations
New York, NY 10017
(212) 963-8093
website: www.unep.org

UNEP's mandate is to provide leadership and encourage partnership in caring for the environment by inspiring, informing, and enabling nations and peoples to improve their quality of life without compromising that of future generations. It is an active participant in a wide variety of international research and action plans.

Wildlife Conservation Society (WCS)
185th St. and Southern Blvd.
Bronx, NY 10460
(718) 220-6891

Dedicated to preserving the earth's wildlife and ecosystems, the WCS combines scientifically based conservation efforts in the field with captive propagation of endangered species, and it provides environmental education for local, national, and international audiences.

World Wildlife Fund (WWF)
1250 24th St. NW
Washington, DC 20037
(202) 293-4800
website: www.wwf.org

Established in 1961, the WWF is one of the most well known conservation groups in the world. It helps to create and protect wildlife reserves throughout the world, and develops public education programs, investigates poaching and smuggling, and attempts to reconcile human needs with conservation through research and active programs.

Suggestions for Further Reading

Books

Ruth Ashby, *The Orangutan.* Englewood Cliffs, NJ: Silver Burdett Press, 1994. This is a rather simple yet informative book about the life and habits of Asia's only great ape.

Birute Galdikas, *Reflections of Eden: My Years with the Orangutans of Borneo.* Vol. 1. Boston: Little, Brown, 1996. This book provides a fairly recent account of Galdikas's work in the rain forests of Borneo. She describes the joys and frustrations of dedicating her life to unraveling the mysteries of the reclusive red ape.

Sy Montgomery, *Walking with the Great Apes.* Boston: Houghton Mifflin, 1991. This book chronicles the research conducted on each of the world's great apes: chimpanzees, gorillas, and orangutans. Montgomery focuses on the life's work of Jane Goodall, Dian Fossey, and Birute Galdikas.

J. R. Napier and P. H. Napier, *The Natural History of the Primates.* Cambridge, MA: MIT Press, 1985. This is an overview of all the world's known primates. The book gives a brief account of the biology and behavior of each species. It is full of detailed photographs and provides a good general background on the different family branches of the primate order.

Michael Nichols, *The Great Apes: Between Two Worlds.* Washington, DC: National Geographic Society, 1993. This is an attractive, easy-to-read book. It has short stories on a variety of topics concerning all of the great apes, their behavior, and their relationship with humankind. Each story is complemented by stunning photography.

Periodicals

Birute Galdikas, "Waiting for Orangutans," *Discover,* December 1994.

Bil Gilbert, "New Ideas in the Air at the National Zoo," *Smithsonian,* June 1996.

Steve Kuznik, "How to Be an Orangutan," *International Wildlife,* January/February 1997.

Works Consulted

Books

Aline Amon, *Orangutan: The Endangered Ape.* New York: Atheneum, 1977. This is an account of the life and habits of the orangutan as well as a discussion of some of the issues revolving around its endangered status. It is a fairly old book, so most of the statistics are out of date, but it still provides an easy-to-read account of the red ape's behavior.

L. E. M. de Boer, *The Orangutan: Its Biology and Conservation.* The Hague, Netherlands: W. Junk, 1982. Another book that is slightly old but provides a good general background of the orangutan's biology and behavior. The sections on conservation are somewhat outdated.

A. A. Eudey, *Action Plan for Asian Primate Conservation.* Riverside, CA: IUCN/SSC Primate Specialist Group, 1987. This is a technical account of the Primate Specialist Group's 1987 conservation plan. It includes the results of detailed studies of populations, habitat surveys, and captive-breeding summaries.

Michael Kavanagh, *A Complete Guide to Monkeys, Apes, and Other Primates.* London: Oregon, 1983. This is an interesting textbook that provides a brief account of the biology, behavior, and habitat usage of every primate on earth. It provides illustrations as well as taxonomic maps that illustrate exactly how all of the primates are related.

Terry Maple, *Orangutan Behavior.* New York: Van Nostrand Reinhold, 1980. This is one book in a series by Terry Maple. His other books include *Chimpanzee Behavior* and *Gorilla Behavior.* These books give an interesting account of the early research done on each ape's behavior, both in the wild and in captivity.

Jacqueline J. Ogden, Lorraine A. Perkins, and Lori Sheeran, *The Proceedings of the International Conference on Orangutans: The Neglected Ape.* San Diego: Zoological Society of San Diego, 1994. Notes of conference hosted by the Zoological Society of San Diego, which includes both the San Diego Zoo and the Wild Animal Park. The Society's mission is both the conservation and preservation of endangered species such as the orangutan as well as the education and entertainment of visitors from around the world.

Jeffrey H. Schwartz, *The Red Ape: Orang-utans and Human Origins.* Boston: Houghton Mifflin, 1987. In addition to the basic summary of the orangutan's biology and behavior, this book deals with Schwartz's own personal belief that orangutans are more closely related to humans than any other ape. The author provides some interesting arguments for his unconventional ideas.

Victoria J. Taylor and Nigel Dunstone, eds., *The Exploitation of Mammal Populations.* London: Chapman & Hall, 1996. This book about the plight of mammals worldwide contains a paper entitled "Use, Misuse, and Abuse of the Orang-utan."

Periodicals

Associated Press, "US and World Report: Indonesia—Orangutans," November 11, 1997.

John Bonner, "Taiwan's Tragic Orang-utans," *New Scientist,* December 3, 1994.

Karen Freeman, "Rescue of Besieged Orangutans Aids Research," *New York Times,* November 4, 1997.

Thomas Fuller, "Forests Die as Borneo Prays for Rain," *International Herald Tribune,* April 20, 1998.

Joshua Hammer, "A Typhoon in a Rainforest Eden," *Newsweek,* June 1, 1998.

Simon Husson, "On the Move," *Geographical Magazine,* June 1996.

International Wildlife, "Should We Put Them All Back?" September/October 1993.

Jakarta Post, "Fire Damage Losses Rise to Rp. 8.27 Trillion: Report," April 27, 1998.

Kenneth Miller and Alan Sheldon, "Saving the Last Orangutans," *Life,* May 1998.

Mary Morse, "Orangutan Alert: Deforestation and Poaching Imperil Our Ape Cousins," *Utne Reader,* July/August 1993.

Seth Mydans, "In Vast Forest Fires of Asia, Scant Mercy for Orangutans," *New York Times,* December 16, 1997.

The Politics of Extinction: The Orangutan Crisis/The Destruction of Indonesia's Forests. London: Environmental Investigation Agency, 1998.

Janet Raloff, "Caste-Off Orangs," *Science News,* March 25, 1995.

Linda Spalding, "The Jungle Took Her," *Outside,* May 1998.

Mark Starowicz, "Leakey's Last Angel," *New York Times Magazine,* August 16, 1992.

Ronald Tilson, *Orangutan Population and Habitat Viability Analysis Report.* Indonesia: IUCN's Species Survival Commission, October 23, 1993.

Internet Sources

Balikpapan Orangutan Society, "About the Rainforest." www.redcube.nl/bos/forest.htm.

———, "Orangutans at Risk." www.redcube.nl/bos/bos.htm.

———, "Research at Wanariset Station." www.redcube.nl/bos/research.htm.

———, "Threats to the Orangutan." www.redcube.nl/bos/news.htm.

Rachel Drewry, "Ecotourism: Can It Save the Orangutan?" *Inside Indonesia.* www.serve.com/inside/.

World Wildlife Fund (press release), "Indonesian Fires' Distress Leads People to Kill Orangutans," October 30, 1997. www.panda.org/news/press/news_161.htm.

Index

Picture Credits

Cover photo: © Digital Stock
AFP/Corbis, 88
© Toni Angermayer/Photo Researchers, 24
AP/Wide World Photos, 80
© Bob Bennett/The Wildlife Collection, 5, 10 (right)
    Jonathan Blair/Corbis, 63
Rodney Brindamour/National Geographic Image Collection,
    14, 30
W. Perry Conway/Corbis, 26, 29, 34, 73, 84, 92
Corbis, 60
Corbis-Bettmann, 50, 65, 76
Digital Stock, 59
Gerry Ellis/ENP Images, 11, 16, 18, 25, 36, 38, 40
© Michael H. Francis/The Wildlife Collection, 19
Mitchell Gerber/Corbis, 79
© Martin Harvey/The Wildlife Collection, 10 (left), 45
Hulton-Deutsch Collection/Corbis, 32, 69
Dan Lamont/Corbis, 44
Wayne Lawler; Ecoscene/Corbis, 46
Lineworks, Incorporated, 8
© Mark Newman/Tom Stack & Associates, 37, 48
PhotoDisc, 52, 77, 81, 94
© Larry Tackett/Tom Stack & Associates, 13
Michael S. Yamashita/Corbis, 72, 90

About the Author

Stuart P. Levine received his bachelor's degree in psychology at Binghamton University in New York, and his associate's degree in wildlife education and animal training at Moorpark College in southern California. He has spent most of his career training animals for educational outreach programs, geared towards heightening people's awareness about conservation. Levine currently resides in central Florida and has written two other books in Lucent's Endangered Animals and Habitats series: *The Elephant* and *The Tiger.*